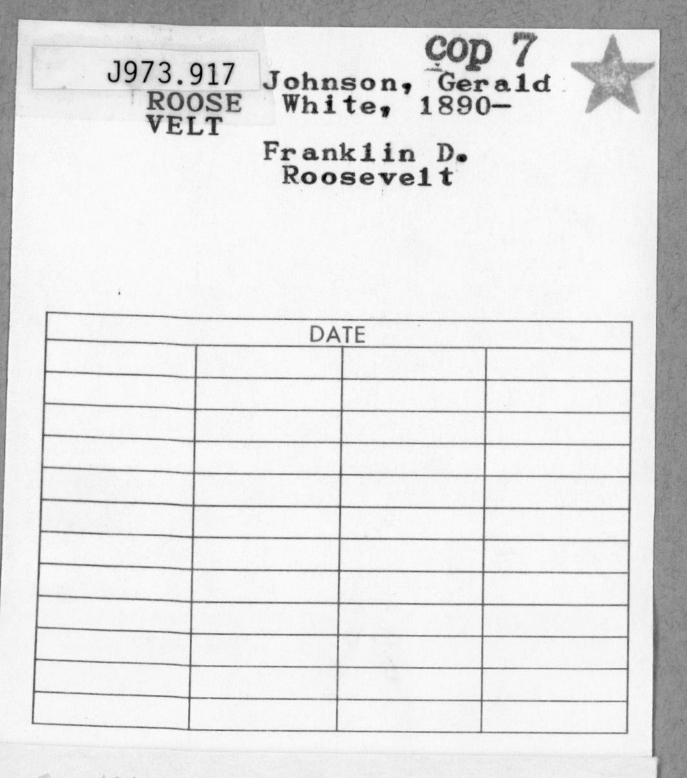
cop 7
J973.917
ROOSE
VELT
Johnson, Gerald
White, 1890-
Franklin D.
Roosevelt
DATE

# FRANKLIN D. ROOSEVELT

## PORTRAIT OF A GREAT MAN

# FRANKLIN D. ROOSEVELT

## PORTRAIT OF A GREAT MAN

BY GERALD W. JOHNSON

illustrated with 30 photographs
decorations by Leonard Everett Fisher

William Morrow and Company
New York 1967

*Acknowledgments for Photographs*

Franklin D. Roosevelt Library, frontispiece, 15, 21, 25, 30, 39, 47, 82, 87, 88, 103, 121, 167, 170, 173, 174, 175, 177, 179
Harris & Ewing, 75
United Press International, 73, 126, 129, 135, 140, 159, 161, 182
Wide World Photos, 132


Published simultaneously in Canada by George J. McLeod Limited, Toronto.
Printed in the United States of America.
Library of Congress Catalog Card Number AC 67-10579

# CONTENTS

# Illustrations

# AUTHOR'S NOTE

From the time he was elected governor of New York until his death, the story of Franklin Delano Roosevelt is very nearly the history of the United States and a large part of the history of the world. Several historians, notably Freidel and the younger Schlesinger, have written many volumes about his life without pretending to include everything he did and said and thought, and there are literally hundreds of other books about him and his part in great events.

In this book no attempt will be made to tell the whole story. Much of it does not help us to understand Roosevelt, for usually he did what he had to do, what any other man in his high office would have had to do. But there were a few instances in which the kind of man he was decided the kind of thing he did, and those events are the ones I have tried to select for this biography.

*Gerald W. Johnson*
*Baltimore, Maryland*
*July, 1966*

CHAPTER I

# THE ROOSEVELT FAMILY

Sometimes a boy who has everything grows up into a man who is nothing, or nothing that people can remember. But it doesn't always happen that way. Once there was a boy, born in 1882, named Franklin Delano Roosevelt, who had a great deal. In the first place, his family had enough money. There were many richer families in New York, but the Roosevelts were not poor, and the children had everything they really needed: nice houses to live in, nice clothes to wear, nice people among their friends, good schools, and good teachers. They had time to play and places where they could play. Franklin had a bicycle and a pony and, when he grew old enough, a sailboat of his own.

The Roosevelts were an unusual family. In two ways they were very American indeed. In two other ways they were very different from most Americans. They were American in the sense that they had been in America a long time; the exact year in which the first Roosevelt landed in this country is not known, but it was about 1636. They were also American in that they never thought it mattered much where they came from. The first Roosevelt was Dutch and so was his wife, but his sons, grandsons, great-grandsons, and so on, paid little attention to that. When a Roosevelt met a girl he liked he married her, not caring whether her family was English, French, Italian, Swedish, or anything else. President Roosevelt thought he was about one-seventh Dutch. Since most old American families are of mixed ancestry, the Roosevelts were like the rest.

But they were different from most families in that they had always known how to take care of money. Some of them also knew how to make money, but that ability is not exactly the same thing. The first Roosevelt, whose name was Claes Martenszan van Rosenvelt, and his son, who called himself Nicholas Roosevelt, were farmers. In those early days land was not hard to get, although plenty of hard work was needed to make a living on the land. Both father and son seem to have been hard-working, respectable people who did pretty well, but not well enough to be exciting. The grandson, however, went into the sugar-refining business, and by the time of the Revolution he was a prominent businessman in the little town that was New York in 1776. His children, and his children's children kept the family's wealth. They were not stingy. Many of them gave to charity, but they didn't waste money, and the Roosevelts have had money ever since. In this way they were different from most American families.

A second way in which they were different was that they stayed close to where they first landed—New York. Most American families have moved about. For many years there was free land to be had in the West, and even today young men move from place to place when they think they can find a better job somewhere else. But the Roosevelts stayed put, not all in New York City, but not far away. Franklin's branch of the family centered at Hyde Park, which is just up the Hudson River from the city.

Franklin's father, James Roosevelt, was a good and wise man. He was also a quiet man, who never made much stir in the world, mild and gentle most of the time, but when a question of right and wrong arose he was as hard as a rock. He taught his son that there are some things that a gentleman cannot do, even though there is no law against them, and one of them is to be rude to people who mean no harm.

He did something far more important than teach his son good manners, however. James Roosevelt set an example of living neither idly nor lavishly. He hoped that the boy would work, but not to make a great fortune. There are many things worth doing that bring in little or no money, so men who have to make a living cannot afford to take such jobs; but a man whose living is already taken care of can.

James himself was such a man. His own father had left him some money, and he had a business office in New York where he made more, but not a great deal more. He was no better than a moderately good businessman, because his heart really wasn't in the work, and he gave much of his time to things that brought in no money, but gave him satisfaction. He lived on his country place at Hyde Park, overlooking the Hudson River near Poughkeepsie; and there he was for years a member of the school board, a vestryman of the Episcopal church, active in various projects for the public good, and in experiments on his farm to improve the soil and introduce new plants that might be valuable. His neighbors once tried to get him to run for Congress, but that he would not do, because he would have had to give up his work for the neighborhood.

He was liked and respected in Dutchess County, which is where Hyde Park is located, and he was liked and respected in New York City. That was all he wanted. He cared nothing for great fame or great fortune and he hoped his son would follow his example.

But Franklin had a mother, as well as a father, and she was a different kind of person. Mrs. James Roosevelt, born Sara Delano, had a great influence on the boy. In some ways it was the opposite kind of influence, and because she lived many years after James's death, some people think it was far stronger. They believe that Franklin paid more attention to his mother than to anybody else. They may be right.

Franklin in Scottish kilts, January, 1887

In a way, they were certainly right, for nobody could stay around Sara Delano Roosevelt without paying some attention to her. She was the kind of woman that demands attention, a managing woman, and she did her best to manage her son, especially after her husband died.

This is not to say that she was a bad mother. On the contrary, she loved her son with all her heart and was, perhaps, a little too good to him. Still, she had strong ideas about things that she considered bad for small boys, and when she said no, that was the end of the discussion.

Indeed, Sara had strong ideas about everything. She came from a strong-minded family. Her first American ancestor was Philippe de la Noye, who landed in Plymouth apparently some years before Claes Martenszan van Rosenvelt reached New York. De la Noye was strong-minded enough to be a Huguenot, that is, a Protestant in Catholic France, and to take his chances with the Puritans in the American wilderness when Jamestown was only fourteen years old. But perhaps the strongest-minded of the lot was Philippe's great-great-great grandson, Warren, by whose time the name had become Delano. Warren Delano made a fortune as a shipowner trading with the Far East, then he lost most of it in the great panic of 1857. Thereupon he went to Hong Kong in 1859 and made another, mostly in opium, for which there was a great demand in the military hospitals during the Civil War. This time Warren Delano invested his money safely and bought a place near Hyde Park, where James Roosevelt lived.

They first met in a business way, but later became friends.

"Mr. Roosevelt is the first man who showed me that a Democrat can be a gentleman," said Warren Delano. But apparently Roosevelt never met Delano's five beautiful daughters until he was fifty-two years old and his first wife had been dead for some years. Then he met Sara, who was twenty-six, and promptly fell in love. Warren Delano was disgusted; he thought Roosevelt much too old, but Sara had a mind as strong as her father's and she had made it up. So Warren gave in, and it was well that he did for the marriage turned out to be a happy one.

# CHAPTER II

## GROTON

As a small boy Franklin seemed to be not very different from his fifteen or twenty cousins of about the same age. He was as bright as the others, but not so much brighter as to be a boy wonder. Perhaps he studied his lessons harder than most, but not very much harder. His teachers called him a good average. He liked the things that boys usually like: games, his pony, and above all, his sailboat. He collected things—minerals and shells and stamps—and like most boys he switched from one to another. The exception was stamps; all his life he liked to collect stamps.

In only one way was Franklin different from some of the other children in the family: he never went to public school. When he was small he was taught by governesses, and when he grew up a bit by tutors. One summer, when his parents were in Europe, he attended a German school, and, to prepare for college, he went to Groton, a private school for boys in Massachusetts.

This kind of education was fine in some ways, but in other ways it was not so good. Groton at that time was regarded as one of the best schools in America, and so it was, as far as the teaching was concerned. No teacher could hold a job at Groton unless, first, he knew his subject and, second, he knew how to teach it. The headmaster was Reverend Doctor Endicott Peabody, very learned, very good, and very strict. A boy at Groton had to work or get out, but because his teachers knew their business they could usually make the work interesting. Doctor Peabody was strict, but he was fair, so most of the boys liked him even if they were a little afraid of him, and those that didn't like him respected him.

But there were two things about Groton that made it not so good a school for a boy who was to go into American politics. Doctor Peabody was a member of a family that had been in Massachusetts slightly longer than the Roosevelts had been in New York, but they hadn't married wives of so many different nations. They had remained almost entirely English with much respect for the English way of life. Endicott Peabody was educated at an English college, Cheltenham, and he always believed that the best type of

English gentleman is about the finest kind of man in the world. So in his school he tried to make the boys as much like English gentlemen as he could. The idea wasn't bad, except that these boys were Americans, and the more like Englishmen they became, the less like Americans they were.

The second objection was that all, or nearly all, the boys at Groton were exactly like Franklin Roosevelt in that they came from families with plenty of money—for Groton was quite expensive—and they always had everything that they really needed. Now one of the most interesting things about the United States is the great number of different kinds of people there are in the country. There were about seventy-five million Americans when Franklin Roosevelt went to school. Only a few were very rich. A few more, but still only a few, were rich enough to send a boy to Groton. Some millions were very poor, and many millions who were not terribly poor still had to do without things the Groton boys enjoyed.

This exclusiveness didn't matter too much if a boy hoped to become a lawyer or a doctor or to go into business or to become a scholar or a churchman. But for a politician it was very bad training. A politician needs to know all kinds of people, because he can't get elected unless all kinds of people vote for him and, after he is elected, his duty is to do what is best for all the people, not just one class or one party or one religious group. But how can he know what is best for all unless he knows them all, or at least so many kinds that he can pretty well guess what the others need?

However, it is not fair to blame Franklin's mother and

Franklin with his father and mother, May, 1899

father for sending him to a private school such as Groton. Going into politics was the last thing they expected, or wished, their son to do. Serve on the local school board, yes—James Roosevelt had done so—but he flatly refused to run for Congress. Accept a job in the diplomatic service if it were offered, yes—Franklin's older half brother, James (Rosy) Roosevelt had done so—but he never ran for any elective office. To serve in such public jobs, James thought, was the duty of an American gentleman, although Sara probably had her doubts. They expected Franklin to go into business or the law or possibly some kind of scholarly work, and as preparation for these careers Groton was excellent. They honestly believed that they were doing their very best for their son, and they would have been right—if things had turned out as they expected.

There is no reason to doubt that Franklin thought the same way, if he thought about the choice of school at all, which he probably did not. Why should he? Everybody he knew, of his own age, was going to Groton, or to some place like it, and afterward to Harvard or Yale or perhaps Princeton. A small boy doesn't usually question being called upon to do what the rest of the gang are doing.

So he went along without objecting but, as far as we know, without getting much excited about his education. After all, he had been around quite a lot. James and Sara Roosevelt both liked to travel, and when Franklin was very young they went to Europe nearly every year. At home James was a director of a railroad, which meant that when the family traveled in this country they traveled in style, especially when James was going to some meeting of railroad men and had a private car offered him. On many of these trips he took his wife and son with him, so by the time he reached his teens Franklin had seen a good deal of this country as well as of Europe.

One of these trips he remembered vividly as long as he lived. James had business in Washington and took his son along. While there they called at the White House, for the President of the United States at that time was Grover Cleveland, who had formerly been governor of New York and was a friend of the Roosevelts. At the moment Mr. Cleveland was having a very bad time. Something he had said or done had enraged his enemies and they were saying the meanest things they could think of about him. Some men he thought were his good friends had turned against him and were making trouble between him and Congress. Some of his pet schemes had gone wrong, and some had been defeated before they could get a start. So the President that day was a sad and tired man. Just as the Roosevelts were leaving he said to the boy, "I have just one wish for you. Pray to God that He will never let you be President of the United States."

But nobody dreamed of what was to come when Franklin set out for boarding school. Most people saw him as a nice boy, but nothing special. Perhaps his mother thought he was a wonder, but most mothers with an only son can see things in him that nobody else can see, so what Sara Roosevelt thought hardly counted.

Her opinion certainly didn't count at Groton, where

young Roosevelt was looked on as pretty much the same as hundreds of other boys who had passed through the school. He was a fairly good student. He always got a passing mark and usually it was a little better than the average of his class, but not so much better as to make his teachers suspect that they had a genius in him. He was growing like a weed and plainly he would be, like his father, a tall man. But, like most boys who are growing fast, he was on the skinny side. For any sport, such as football, which requires beef, he was much too light. He had neither the batting eye, the pitching arm, nor the speed on the paths that make a star baseball player. At tennis he was not bad, but a long way from being a champion. So in athletics, as in the classroom, he was just one of the crowd.

The remarkable thing is that at Groton he was not very popular. Nobody hated him, the other boys just didn't think about him, one way or the other; and, as far as we can tell now, he didn't think much about them. At least, he never made any bosom friends at the school. He seems to have felt that Groton was one of those things to be gone through in order to reach something more important. Anyhow, he left a record at Groton that was not very bad and not very good, just average. It is hard to believe about Franklin D. Roosevelt, but it is so.

During his last year at Groton, when he was seventeen, in 1899, Franklin really buckled down to work. He did more than he had to, for he had already made the credits required for college entrance. So in his last year he took what was, for the most part, really first-year college work.

Roosevelt (seated second from left) with the Groton football teams, 1899

In fact, he won one of the prizes given at the end of the school year—the prize for the best Latin scholar.

The fact that Franklin Roosevelt began to put in some really hard work at seventeen doesn't mean that he had turned into a grind. He was beginning to take much interest in history, especially American history, but to get him really excited one should have offered him, not a book of history, but a sailboat.

About boats he really knew a great deal and was always trying to learn more. James Roosevelt had been sailing boats ever since he was a young man, and he had a fine one at his summer place on Campobello, a Canadian island off the coast of Maine. Long ago Franklin had outgrown his first little boat, which he was not allowed to have until he had sailed with his father or with some person older than he for more than two years, and now he was able to handle his father's big one. During many summers at Campobello he spent most of his time on the water. He learned to know every rock and reef and harbor for many miles around. He knew about tides and currents. He knew exactly what to expect when the wind blew from a certain direction, how to trim his sails, and how to steer the most efficient course. He began to win races, and he knew how to come safely through nasty weather. At seventeen he was a real sailor.

# CHAPTER III

## THEODORE ROOSEVELT

Franklin had a distant cousin, Theodore, who was quite different from the rest of the family. He had started life as a spindly youth, with weak eyes and afflicted with asthma, a disease even yet not fully understood. Many of the family didn't expect him to live long and thought he would be an invalid, or nearly an invalid, while he did live. But he fooled them. Somehow he fought off the asthma and became a strong, vigorous man, a fine horseman, a tennis player, a boxer, and a hunter. Although he had to wear thick glasses, he became an excellent shot with a rifle, and on a cross-country hike he could hold his own with many an athlete.

At Harvard Theodore Roosevelt was a first-rate student, especially interested in history. After college he wrote books of travel, lives of several famous men, and a history, *The Winning of the West,* which ran to four volumes and was a great popular success.

After an unhappy venture as a cattleman in the West, Theodore came back East and plunged into New York City politics, much to the disgust of the more old-fashioned Roosevelts, who were inclined to sniff at politics as no business for a gentleman. Perhaps the sniffing was partly due to the fact that Theodore was a Republican, while most of the Roosevelts had always been Democrats. But Theodore paid no heed. He proved to be a first-rate vote getter, and when war with Spain broke out in 1898, he was Assistant Secretary of the Navy.

The fight between the United States and King Alfonso XIII of Spain was over in three months. In two fast and furious battles, one in Manila Bay, in the Philippine Islands, the other off Santiago, on the island of Cuba, the United States Navy almost completely destroyed the Spanish Navy, and without a navy the king of Spain had no chance to hold on to islands in the Atlantic or the Pacific. The small Spanish Army in the Philippines surrendered almost immediately. The larger one in Cuba fought briefly, but gave up after a few weeks.

At the start Americans believed the war had two aims. One was to avenge the blowing up of our battleship, *Maine,* in Havana harbor, to which it had been sent to protect

Americans during the fighting in Cuba. The other was to help the Cubans throw off Spanish misrule and become an independent nation.

On these two points nearly everyone was agreed. Later we realized that we had no real proof that the Spaniards had blown up the *Maine,* but someone certainly did, and in a Spanish harbor. The Cubans had been fighting for years against a bad colonial government, and to help them seemed right and proper. So men who were to be candidates of the Republican and Democratic parties in 1900 took part in the war. William Jennings Bryan commanded a volunteer infantry regiment. Theodore Roosevelt threw up his job in Washington and helped Leonard Wood organize a regiment of volunteer cavalry. The unit was officially called the First United States Volunteer Cavalry, but people called it the Rough Riders. Bryan's regiment never got to Cuba, so most people soon forgot that he ever served, but Roosevelt's got there in time to take part in a fight at San Juan Hill, which made Roosevelt a national hero.

In the whole war the United States Army had 369 men killed, the Navy 10, and the Marines 6. Against 53,000 killed in World War I, and 291,000 killed in World War II, even against 33,000 killed in Korea, the Spanish-American War looks like a mere skirmish, but its effects were tremendous.

For one thing, it shocked Europe. Many Europeans believed that any one of the five great powers—England, France, Spain, Russia, and Germany—could easily whip any other country except another great power. So when the

Theodore Roosevelt (seated fifth from left) with officers of the Rough Riders, 1898

United States undertook to fight Spain several prominent European statesmen thought it suicide. As a matter of fact, a good many Americans were badly frightened, for the Spanish Navy had three times as many warships as ours. What people failed to take into account was that the Spanish Navy had long been neglected, while the American ships were new and their crews well-trained.

Then when we sent the Spanish Navy to the bottom of the sea in only two real battles, Europe suddenly discovered that here was a sixth great power. It seemed to have come out of nowhere, for Europeans had not paid much attention to what had been going on in this country since the Civil War. But there it was, and its appearance upset all kinds of calculations.

If Europeans were shocked, Americans were startled. We had not dreamed of so swift and easy a victory, and it rather went to our heads. Only half of our success was due to our strength. The other half was due to Spanish weakness. For one thing, their gunners had not been given enough target practice, so many of their shots went wild, while almost all of ours were accurate. But a man who has just won a fight doesn't like to admit, even to himself, that he won partly because his opponent was really a pretty poor fighter.

So in 1898 Americans of the more foolish kind decided that since we beat Spain easily we could beat anybody. President William McKinley knew better, and so did the wiser men among his advisers, but there were some in Congress and in various high offices who were so cocky that they would have been willing to fight all Europe.

One of the leaders of this group was Theodore Roosevelt. He had made such a record in Cuba that he was elected governor of New York in November, 1898. But one who wanted no part of this militancy was James Roosevelt, and Franklin agreed with his father.

Then, in 1900, Theodore was nominated for Vice-President on the Republican ticket with McKinley, who was running for a second term as President. The Democrats nominated Bryan, who had run and lost in 1896, for President. Since James Roosevelt had opposed Bryan earlier, quitting the Democratic party temporarily and voting for McKinley, this nomination might have given him and his son an excuse to support the ticket that had a Roosevelt on it. Franklin was still too young to vote, but he was old enough to take an interest in politics and to argue with the other boys, which he did. However, when Bryan made his principal campaign issue anti-imperialism, that is to say, no colonies, James Roosevelt voted for him, and Franklin shouted for Bryan too, even though a Roosevelt was running for Vice-President on the other ticket.

All the same, when Bryan was beaten and McKinley was reelected President with Theodore Roosevelt as Vice-President, Franklin was very much interested. No doubt he was pleased to have a Roosevelt, and one whom he knew, in what most people considered the second job in the government. To him, it must have seemed that Cousin Theodore simply marched from victory to victory, from one big job to a bigger one, the unbeaten and unbeatable champion. Although Cousin Theodore was a Republican, Franklin no doubt consoled himself with the thought that nobody is perfect. Anyhow, he admired his kinsman tremendously.

That admiration pulled against his father's influence in one respect. James thought that the quiet life of a country gentleman is about the best life anyone can live. Theodore despised it. He was all for the unquiet life—his own term was "the strenuous life"—and he proved that it could be a successful one. But James was successful too, in his own way. So Franklin knew two men who were fine and successful, both of whom he admired; but they held opposite ideas of what makes a good life.

In any case, it is a safe guess that when Franklin found one of his cousins, bearing the same name, had become Vice-President of the United States, he began taking a lively interest in government and probably did more thinking about it than he had ever done before.

However, he soon had sad reason to think about other things. All summer James Roosevelt's health had been failing so badly that he had to give up sailing, and his son took out the family boat alone. In September Franklin was entering Harvard. Shortly before the opening of college James did manage to go along with his wife to Cambridge to help Franklin pick out the furniture and decorations for the room he was to occupy as a student. But not long after that James Roosevelt had to keep to the house, and then to his bed, and on December 8, 1900, he died.

There is no doubt that Franklin Roosevelt felt his father's death deeply, although he didn't say much about it. He never was one to make a great show of his feelings, except when something or somebody made him furious. But we can judge his feeling about his father from the way he referred to James Roosevelt many years later. To the day of his own death he never spoke of his father except with love and pride.

# CHAPTER IV

# HARVARD

Harvard was a new world for Franklin Roosevelt. There he first began to know, not just with the top of his mind, but deep down, that people, far from being all alike, are endlessly different. He found that some people who were entirely different from himself and his friends were yet able and well worth knowing. That discovery comes to many boys during their years in college, and it is one good reason for going to college.

There is some reason to believe that Franklin began this part of his education in reverse gear. Apparently he first learned that some people might belong to his own group and yet be a long way from nice. We know that he wrote home in 1900 that there was at Harvard another Roosevelt, who didn't add credit to the name. This relative, closer in kin to Franklin than to Theodore, was a waster. He gave more of his time to drinking and gambling than he did to studying, and when he was drunk he made a disagreeable fool of himself. In the end he got entangled with a girl and his family took him home, but not before he had caused Franklin much embarrassment. He was afraid that people, knowing of their kinship, would think that therefore they must be alike. This experience taught him two things that he never forgot. One was that being born into a good family doesn't make a boy a gentleman; he has to become one himself. The other was that a man of sense is very careful about alcoholic drinks, for they are tricky.

In his freshman year at Harvard Franklin Roosevelt began to show one quality of a successful man. He developed the ability to stop worrying over what he couldn't get and to turn his mind to making the best of what he had. Almost every healthy college student would like to be a star athlete, and in that desire Roosevelt was like the rest. But, again like most of the others, he didn't have what it takes. At several sports he was not bad, but between being not bad and being a star there is a big difference.

He tried out for nearly everything, and he did make one scrub football team. But, although he was now six feet one and a half inches tall, he weighed only one hundred and forty-six pounds, which was much too light for the varsity.

He was not fast enough for track, and basketball, invented in 1891, had not yet become a major college sport. He made the Freshman Glee Club, but lost out to better voices in his sophomore year.

Only one failure, however, seems to have made much impression on him. Harvard has a number of exclusive and somewhat snobbish student clubs, one of the swankiest of which was the Porcellian, to which Theodore Roosevelt had belonged. Naturally Franklin wished to become a member, too, but he was never elected. What made this failure sting worse than the others was his feeling that it was not his fault. He always believed that he was left out because some of that other Roosevelt's reputation for wildness had rubbed off on him. He was elected to other clubs, some equally exclusive, but the Porcellian had been Theodore's, and it was the one he wanted.

In one tryout, however, he was successful. He made the staff of the *Crimson,* the student newspaper. For the kind of man he was to become this achievement was far more important than membership on any athletic team. As a reporter for the newspaper he had to find out what was going on, and to do so he had to get out and mingle with people, not only with his group of special friends, but with all sorts of people in all departments of the university.

A newspaper reporter, if he is any good, cannot pick and choose the people with whom he will associate. He must find the people who make the news, and they may be anybody. True, the *Crimson,* as a student newspaper, did not try to cover the whole city of Cambridge, much less Boston, across the Charles River. But a university as big as Harvard has within its own walls many different kinds of people. There are students and teachers, to begin with, but there are also scholars doing all sorts of special work. There are doctors and lawyers, and to take care of the university's very large business affairs there must be able businessmen. There are clerks and secretaries and cooks and waiters and gardeners and garbage collectors. Any of these people at any time may do something that is news, if it is only to get run over by a laundry truck. So a reporter on the student newspaper must learn how to talk to all of them, so as to find out what happened.

Certainly some of these people were of a kind that young Roosevelt had never met before. But as he mingled with them he found that many were likeable and that some were to be admired. We know that he liked many by the surest of all tests—they liked him. This conclusion must be true, because every year that Roosevelt was at Harvard he was elected to some kind of office, and in most years to more than one. In his last year he was an editor of the *Crimson.*

At Groton Franklin got along well enough with the other boys, but he didn't stand out from the crowd. He seemed to be just a nice boy, perhaps a little brighter than the average, but in no way startling. One might have thought that any of a dozen other boys would become a more famous man than young Roosevelt. At Harvard, however, signs began to appear that he was not one of the crowd, that he could lead.

One event that may have helped young Roosevelt begin

to pick up the quality of leadership at Harvard occurred in September, 1901. In that month a crazy anarchist murdered President McKinley, and Theodore Roosevelt became President of the United States. That development was a stunner. It far outshone anything any Roosevelt had done since old Claes van Rosenvelt came over from Holland.

Some of the older Roosevelts may have been doubtful about Theodore still, but the younger members of the family were tremendously proud and excited, and he became their idol. Even Franklin admitted that Theodore was the greatest Roosevelt ever heard of, and in 1901 he began to wonder if another Roosevelt could outshine even Theodore.

But with all these outside interests Roosevelt never forgot that he went to college to be educated. From the very start he took as many subjects as the college authorities would allow, and more than they advised students to take. But he was strong and healthy and didn't mind work; as long as he continued to make passing marks, the college did not insist that he slow down. He finished almost all the requirements for a B.A. degree in three years, so most of his fourth year was spent doing more work than was required in subjects that he found especially interesting.

These subjects were for the most part in history. He had always liked history, and because he also liked the sea and boats, he had a great interest in naval history and in the lives of the great sea captains and explorers. By the time he finished at Harvard he knew a great deal about the history of the United States Navy, and he continued to read about

Roosevelt, in 1904, sailing around Campobello Island with his mother

it all the rest of his life until he became a real expert on that subject. There is no doubt that one reason for this interest was the many summers he had spent sailing around Campobello Island and all up and down the New England coast. But perhaps another was the fact that his cousin Theodore was very much an Army man. Franklin admired Theodore and wished he could be such a man, but he did not care to be a copycat. Both were born leaders, but if Theodore at times wanted to be a general, Franklin decided that he would prefer to be an admiral.

But while he was a fairly good student, Franklin Roosevelt never felt any desire to become a historian or, indeed, a scholar of any kind. He did not have that kind of mind. A great scholar is a man who knows all that is known about one subject. There are, however, some men with fine minds who are interested in so many things that they can never settle down to become a real master of any one. Both Roosevelts had minds of that type. In the main, however, Theodore was the more interested in nature, Franklin in people. Before he died Theodore knew an amazing amount about birds, beasts, reptiles, plants, minerals, rivers, mountains, and deserts. Franklin, before he died, knew less about those things, but more about what makes people think and act as they do. That is to say, Theodore was the better scientist, Franklin the better politician.

However, the young man who got his diploma from Harvard in the Class of 1904 was as yet a long way from being a master of men. He was simply a nice young fellow: handsome, intelligent without being a mental giant, amiable, and full of bounce. If the people present on that commencement day had been asked, doubtless most of them would have predicted that young Roosevelt would do well and go far; but probably most of them would have picked several others out of the same class who, they thought, would do better and go farther.

Today that judgment sounds absurd. But if people thought so in 1904 they were neither foolish nor wrong. If Franklin Roosevelt had remained what he was, or had continued along the line he was following that day, it is likely that half a century later nobody could see much difference between him and fifty other Roosevelts who had lived and died before him.

Not that there was anything wrong in what he was or in the way he was going in 1904. His conduct and his course were both most respectable. He probably broke the rules occasionally, but nobody ever heard of his doing anything really scandalous. If he had gone on that way, he would have been a good, solid citizen, respected by his neighbors and on the whole a credit to the family. But when he died he would have been remembered not much longer than the time the pallbearers took to go home, take off their white gloves, and resume their regular business.

Years after he left college he found somewhere the driving power that made him a great leader of men. Even in his youth, no doubt, the seeds of greatness were in him; but that they would grow and finally bear flower and fruit was by no means certain in 1904.

Shakespeare wrote, "Some are born great, some achieve greatness, and some have greatness thrust upon them." It is hard to believe that Franklin D. Roosevelt was born great. If he had been, he would not be half as interesting. The drama of his story is the way by which he in part achieved greatness, and in part had it thrust upon him in the roughest and most painful way.

CHAPTER V

# ELEANOR ROOSEVELT

The most important thing that Franklin D. Roosevelt did after he left Harvard was not, as most people thought, to study law. It was to marry a girl who already bore his own name, for she was a distant cousin and a niece of Theodore. She was Anna Eleanor Roosevelt.

The curious thing is that many, if not quite all, of his friends and relations thought the marriage a mistake. Certainly his mother did, but that reaction is no wonder, for many a mother of an only son fancies that no girl in the world is good enough for her boy. But in this case the mother was not alone in her opinion, and the person who was most terribly afraid that it was a mistake was Eleanor herself.

She was a nice girl, to be sure, but Franklin at twenty-two was not only the best-looking boy in the whole crowd, he was gay and charming and enormously popular. All the girls and their mothers saw him as perhaps the catch of the season. Eleanor, on the other hand, was not at all pretty, not very rich, not witty and gay, but serious-minded, shy, and retiring. Her childhood had been unhappy, and it had left its mark on her. Her father, Elliott Roosevelt, younger brother of Theodore, was a kindly, good-humored fellow who loved his daughter, and she adored him. But he had a fatal weakness. He was a heavy drinker, and the habit killed him while Eleanor was still a child.

Perhaps one reason why he drank to excess was the fact that he had married a woman who had great beauty but not much else. She was Anna Hall, and she came from a family of beautiful women and handsome men. But the women—or at least Eleanor's mother and grandmother—were coldhearted, and the men—or at least two of Eleanor's uncles—were drunkards. When her mother saw that the little girl would never be one of the beautiful Halls, she called her Granny and made fun of her. However, she, too, died before Eleanor was ten, and the child went to her Grandmother Hall, who was not much better. She had been too easygoing with her own children, and she made up for this laxness by being terribly strict with her grandchild. Her mother and grandmother between them convinced Eleanor that she was not and could never be in the least attractive, and so she became afraid to meet people.

When she was fifteen, in 1899, she went to a teen-age dance at a relative's house. Her grandmother had made her wear a dress suitable only for a little girl, and she was terribly ashamed of it. She was having a miserable time until suddenly the best-looking boy in the room asked her to dance, and she nearly fainted with surprise. Probably he did so out of sheer good-nature, because he saw that the poor girl was having a dull time, and he may never have thought of her again. But from that moment on, Franklin Roosevelt meant something very special to Eleanor.

About that time Grandmother Hall arranged for the only really helpful thing she ever did for her granddaughter. She sent Eleanor to England to a girl's school conducted by a very wise and skillful headmistress. This woman saw that Eleanor had something more important than beauty of face and figure, and she worked to bring it out. She was so successful that three years later, in 1902, the American girl came home still not pretty, but far more sure of herself and able to move gracefully and act calmly in any company.

Franklin took note. He had been seeing the girl around all her life, but only as one of the crowd at family parties and other social affairs, and he had never studied her. Probably the thought had not occurred to him that she had anything worth special study. But now it did, and the more he learned about her the more sure he became that she was something quite out of the ordinary, something very fine. In a few months he was very much in love.

Eleanor, for all her social training in England, had come back still persuaded that she could never be a social success, so she had better find some more serious purpose in life. She belonged to the Junior League, and she went into social work in a wholehearted way. Like Franklin at Harvard, she found that outside her social circle there were vast numbers of people of many different kinds, all of whom were interesting, and some of whom were admirable. The more she found out about this different world, the more fascinating it became.

Yet, for all that, she was a normal young woman with dreams of romance, like any other. The difference was that when romance actually showed up, not in a fairy tale, but in real life, she didn't expect it. She was so free of vanity that she was astonished when she found that this most desirable young man was really serious in asking her to marry him. His proposal made her very happy, but it scared her, too. Many years later, when the romance was all over, and she wrote the story of her own amazing life, she still didn't understand how their marriage happened.

But the world understands, except for one thing. The mystery that remains is how Franklin D. Roosevelt, at the age of twenty-two, could be so shrewd a judge of character against appearance. Not many young men are able to look beyond the outward appearance and see the real person behind the mask. Usually the experience that comes with more years than twenty-two is needed to make a man understand the meaning of the saying that beauty is only skin deep. Even among her friends at that time few saw anything in Eleanor Roosevelt but a nice, quite ordinary young girl.

But Franklin knew. We can be sure of that fact because of the battle that he had with his mother over the marriage. Sara Roosevelt had nothing special against Eleanor. The girl was wellborn, well-bred, a lady in every respect, and, while not rich, she was not a pauper either. Her father had left her some money, not millions, but what the Roosevelt circle called a decent amount. Sara didn't object to the girl, but she considered her son too young to marry. In this respect, again, she was like many mothers of only sons. If they have their way, they will think their sons too young to marry at any age.

This time Sara didn't have her way, and the fact that she didn't shows something in her son's makeup that puzzled shrewd observers in later years. Up to then, Franklin had given every sign of being, as the saying is, tied to his mother's apron strings. Even when he went to Harvard, Sara, after her husband's death, moved to Cambridge to watch over and look after him. However, Franklin was really more like his father than Sara realized. James Roosevelt was a peaceful soul who would go a long way for a quiet life; but when he put his foot down it stayed down, and Sara knew it. She was as stubborn as any of her Huguenot ancestors, but when in a showdown James was as stubborn as any hardheaded Dutchman from Claes van Rosenvelt down.

When in a pinch Franklin could be as stubborn as the two of them put together. But even more than his father,

Franklin and Eleanor Roosevelt at a cousin's wedding on June 18, 1904

he disliked a row in the household, and he was even smoother than James at devising means of getting his own way without a knockdown fight.

When his mother opposed his marriage, he didn't argue with her. He just went on quietly making preparations. He was in his senior year at college when he proposed to Eleanor, and they agreed that they must wait until he had graduated. When Sara refused to announce the engagement, he didn't try to force her. He cared nothing about the announcement anyhow. When his mother insisted on a cruise in the Caribbean right after commencement, he went along. Eleanor, too, wanted a little time between the graduation and the wedding. All he demanded was that Sara be decently polite to Eleanor, and she would have been so in any case. She was no shrew.

On her part, Eleanor did everything she could think of to placate her future mother-in-law, and gradually they wore down the old lady. It must be said for Sara that when she gave up she did so completely. She announced the engagement soon after the Presidential election of 1904, which Theodore won triumphantly, aided by Franklin's vote and the fact that the Democrats had nominated a respectable old stuffed shirt named Parker, instead of their best vote getter, Bryan.

Eleanor and Franklin fixed the wedding date for March 17, 1905, partly because Theodore was to be in New York that day to lead the Saint Patrick's Day parade, and he was to give the bride away. Naturally, it was a big social event. Any wedding that involved the Roosevelts, the Delanos, the Halls, and others of that group would have been a big one. But when, in addition, the bride was to be given in marriage by her uncle, the President of the United States, it was more than big, it was terrific. As matters turned out, the wedding was just that, but in a way that nobody intended. After the ceremony there was the usual reception with the bridal party receiving in one room while in an adjoining room a table was spread with the customary things to eat and drink.

The President, after chatting a few minutes with the newly-weds and their attendants, strolled into the outer room, whereupon all the guests crowded after him. The bridal pair was left alone, and there was nothing to do but trail along after the others. The disruption was certainly not intentional on Theodore Roosevelt's part, for he was fond of Eleanor, and years later Mrs. Roosevelt could laugh about it, but at the time it stung a little. Still, in those days any place where Theodore Roosevelt happened to be was inevitably the center of attention. He didn't try to make it so. It just happened, because he was not merely the President, he was also an interesting person. There is no doubt, though, that he enjoyed being the center of attention, which made one of his sons say jokingly, "Whenever Father goes to a wedding he wants to be the bride, and whenever he goes to a funeral he wants to be the corpse."

Apparently Eleanor Roosevelt's fate was to do things the hard way, even to getting married. That in one lifetime she did so much then becomes even more remarkable.

# CHAPTER VI

# YOUNG LAWYER

Although Roosevelt's decision to study law after he left Harvard was expected to be very important in making his career, it turned out not to amount to much. Franklin D. Roosevelt was not cut out to be a lawyer. Oh, he did pretty well. He went to the law school of Columbia University and learned enough to get a license and be admitted to the bar. Being a Roosevelt, he had no trouble in joining one of the best law firms in New York. He brought it some business, which pleased the senior partners, and such matters as were turned over to him he handled very well. He could make a living at the law, but his heart wasn't in it; and when a man's heart isn't in it, he never becomes a really big lawyer, the kind that we call a leader of the bar.

The guess is fairly safe that he went into the law, not because he loved it, but because he couldn't think of anything else to do. He did not have to take whatever job he could find to make a living. His father had left him enough money to live on without a job. But his father had also taught him that a man who spends his whole life playing around merely because he doesn't have to work is not much of a man. Franklin Roosevelt had no intention of being a playboy, and he knew that he ought to go into some kind of work in which a good mind and a good education count.

But he had no desire to become a doctor of medicine and, although he was a good churchman, still less to become a doctor of divinity. He could write, but he was not a born writer; he preferred to do things rather than tell about them. He had no special talent for painting or sculpture or music so he could not hope to become an artist. There remained business and the law, but business bored him. So did the law, but not as much, and he felt that he was better at it.

So Roosevelt became a lawyer. The decision pleased his mother, not because she thought highly of lawyers, but because the profession was a gentlemanly one. What she really wished her son to be was a country gentleman living on his estate like an upper-class English landowner. Sara never understood what kind of child she had brought into the world. She had little of his admiration for his cousin. She admitted that Theodore had made a great stir in the world, but making a great stir was something she disliked. Being in the newspapers every day seemed to her somewhat vulgar. True, Theodore in the end had been elected to the highest office in the land, but to do so he had to associate with a great many men whom Sara regarded as low persons with bad manners and, she suspected, worse morals. That sort of life was not for her precious son, and she hoped that practicing law as a member of a most dignified and respectable firm would keep him out of it.

For a while Roosevelt's work did, but not for very long. The kind of law practiced by his firm dealt with things more than with people. If Roosevelt had been in court every day defending some client accused of crime, he might have found the law more interesting. Instead, his business was with contracts, wills, trust funds, buying and selling various kinds of property, organizing corporations. This part of the law is very important, and the lawyer who is good at it can make a great deal of money. Some men like it and not only make money out of it, they have a good time doing so. But it bored Roosevelt.

During those years he also tried two or three business projects. Practically all of these adventures fell into two classes: some were bad and others were worse. None was really good. On the other hand, none was so bad that it ruined him, for he was always careful never to risk all the money he had in one project. He was not what businessmen call a plunger. As regards money he was as careful as any of his Dutch forefathers had been. But his business deals taught him one thing, which was that if he didn't like the law he had better not go into business, for he was not likely to be any more successful there than he was in a law office.

The fact is that at this time Franklin D. Roosevelt was exactly like a great many other young men just out of college. He didn't know what he wanted to do. This lack of purpose may seem a strange thing in one who had a fine mind and as good an education as was to be had, as well as many friends in high places who could help him along. Yet often just such young men have more trouble than most others in deciding what to do. The fellow who is really good at just one thing is not bothered; he bears down on that one thing and often makes a brilliant success of it. But when one is pretty good at almost anything, he may take a long time to discover which is his best line. Sometimes he never discovers it and remains a second-rater all his life.

The twenty-eighth President of the United States, Woodrow Wilson, once wrote an essay about this problem. He called it, "When a Man Comes to Himself," a title that at first glance doesn't seem to make sense. But the essay makes sense. Wilson argued that when a man discovers what he can do best and settles down to do it, he then becomes a full-grown man or "comes to himself." Age is not decisive. Some at seventeen know what they really want to do; some at thirty are still undecided; some live all their lives without finding out.

So all the time that Roosevelt sat in his New York law office racking his brain over deeds and contracts, wills and charters, he wondered what he really wanted to do. He couldn't see that practicing law the way he was doing it was much of a public service. There was nothing wrong about it. It was a perfectly respectable way of life and a necessary service to private business. He remembered how his father had told him that a man who is lucky enough not to have to spend all his time making a living, ought to spend part of his time doing something for the general good, and he could not see that he was doing much of anything along that line.

Then there was always the nagging thought of Theodore. Franklin deplored Theodore's Republicanism and regarded many of his friends and supporters as bad characters. But he did not believe that Theodore had a part in any of their rascalities. On the other hand, the elder Roosevelt had attacked many kinds of crooked dealings in public life and in business, which had been regarded up until then as strictly private life, not to be interfered with by politicians.

This work Franklin believed was a real contribution to the public good, the very kind of thing that James Roosevelt had always insisted was the duty of a gentleman fortunate enough to be able to devote his time and energy to it. Was, then, Theodore stooping when he entered politics? Franklin thought not. Franklin thought that in trying to do some good in the world, Theodore was being more, not less of, a gentleman than those Roosevelts who felt that all the country had a right to ask of a gentleman was that he do no harm.

It is to Roosevelt's credit that he thought so, but we don't have to assume that his desire to serve the country was the only thing that made him dissatisfied with his own life. After all, Theodore lived constantly in the midst of excitement, and at times he held tremendous power. Naturally a vigorous young man likes excitement and wishes for power. Of course Franklin was envious of Theodore, but not with the kind of envy that leads to hatred and malice. His was mixed with admiration and honest pride. But it did increase his feeling that he ought to be doing something more important than drawing up contracts and advising clients how to keep out of legal trouble.

Still, Roosevelt didn't do anything about his dissatisfaction until he had been out of Harvard six years and out of law school three.

CHAPTER VII

# STATE SENATOR

As the Presidential election of 1908 approached Theodore Roosevelt began looking around for a successor who would continue what he had begun. He wouldn't run himself because, after President McKinley was killed in 1901, he had served three years, and he considered those years his first term. His second term ran from 1904 until 1908. While there was no law against serving for three terms, the practice was considered improper.

So Theodore looked around for a man on whom he could rely to act as he had acted in the White House. He chose

William H. Taft, his Secretary of War, and publicly told the Republicans that if they would not nominate Taft, he would run again, third term or no. So all Roosevelt's enemies hastily swung to Taft, and he was nominated and elected.

The choice was a bad one, yet it is easy to understand. Taft was fat, jolly, and slow-moving, but he had a fine mind and was perfectly honest. He had done well as governor-general of the Philippines, and even better as Secretary of War, where, under the direction of the President, he handled the Army's affairs smoothly and well. When he thoroughly understood what needed to be done, there were few men in the country who could do it better or more promptly.

But Taft had never clearly understood what Theodore Roosevelt was trying to do. He didn't know enough about the country. He knew the law. He knew the Philippines. He knew the Army. But he didn't know the wheat and corn growers in the Middle West, or the cotton growers in the South, or the factory hands in the industrial cities. He didn't know how profoundly the country was changing, and, not knowing, he clung to the belief that the old, time-tested ways were best and that changes should be slight and slow.

The old-line Republican leaders in Congress agreed with him. Most of them knew even less about the country than he did. Most of them were better acquainted with bankers and big businessmen than with farmers and factory workers. The system had worked well for them, and they saw no reason to change it. So when Taft came to the Presidency they set about happily undoing most of what Theodore Roosevelt had done.

Unfortunately, not all of them were as honest as Taft. Some were not interested in principle, but only in snatching whatever they could for themselves and their friends. Some of the men Taft appointed to minor offices proved to be very shady characters and some of the laws enacted by Congress were outrageous in the way they gave more riches and power to the already rich and powerful. Roosevelt, who had gone abroad when his term ended to hunt big game in Africa, was aghast when he came back. He felt that his friend, whom he had made President, had betrayed him, which was hardly fair but very natural, and he began to denounce Taft.

All of which gave new life to the Democratic party. Now that the Republicans under Taft had turned their backs on Theodore Roosevelt's ideas, things began to look brighter for the Democrats. In 1910 they put real steam into their effort to capture Congress and as many state legislatures as they could.

This year, when he was twenty-eight years old, Franklin Delano Roosevelt "came to himself," as Woodrow Wilson would have said. He went into politics.

But he did so in a way that was all his own, a way that confused some people and kept them guessing what kind of man he was. A bunch of local politicians, who thought they were smart, decided to use the young man for their own purposes. Roosevelt knew perfectly well what they were up to, but he agreed to go along, and then he used them for his purposes.

Roosevelt's first political campaign happened this way. Hyde Park is in Dutchess County, of which Poughkeepsie is the county seat. In those days Poughkeepsie had a large Democratic vote and could usually elect a member of the assembly, the lower house of the New York legislature. But the state senatorial district included Columbia and Putnam, both farming counties, as well as Dutchess, and the district as a whole was so rock-ribbed Republican that it had elected only one Democrat since 1856. The result was that while Democratic politicians were willing enough to run for assemblyman, a race in which one had a chance of winning, nobody cared to run for state senator, although the office was higher, for the chance of winning was practically zero.

Still, the Democrats had to put up a candidate, if only for the looks of the thing. One of the Poughkeepsie group, a man named Mack, had had some law business with young Roosevelt's law firm, and he had taken a real liking to the young man. So he suggested to the others that they choose him for the nominee. He couldn't win, but he was a fine-looking young fellow, who would make a good impression, and the fact that his name was Roosevelt would draw a few votes. Most important of all, he was supposed to be rich—much richer than he actually was—and might be expected to put up a nice wad of money that would help elect other candidates. He didn't know anything about campaigning, but if he put up the money, what of that? He couldn't win anyhow, so his defeat would be no real loss.

This strategy looked like good sense to all except one man who was a follower of Charles F. Murphy, Democratic boss of New York City. But the deal looked so good to the rest that they argued this man down and offered the nomination to Roosevelt.

He promptly accepted. His mother didn't think much of the idea, and neither did Eleanor, but Eleanor would do whatever Franklin wanted, and his mother had learned that when he had set his head there was no stopping him. So they both agreed, and as the campaign went on Sara became really interested. She even gave some money, although nothing like the huge sums the politicians had dreamed of. She and her son together put up about $2500, which, for a local campaign in 1910, was not to be sniffed at.

The candidate himself, though, was the real sensation. He started out by doing a thing that all the politicians said would kill his chances, if he had ever had any, finally and forever. He hired a big, red automobile, a rarity in those days, with a man to drive it, and set out to visit every farmer in the three counties.

They thought he was crazy. They predicted that when that big, red devil wagon came roaring down a country road, scaring the farmer's horses and probably running over his dogs and chickens, the farmer would reach for his shotgun. Far from getting a vote, the candidate would be lucky not to get a load of bird shot. They said that even if there was no shooting, the candidate would make a terrible impression. When out of the car bounced a grinning young man, well-dressed and well-groomed, his trousers pressed and his shoes shined, the farmer would say to himself, "Here is certainly a city dude and probably a city slicker." Farmers were notorious for not liking either dudes or slickers. The politicians said that at the rate young Roosevelt was carrying on, the Democrats wouldn't get one vote outside the Poughkeepsie city limits.

But the campaign didn't work out that way. What really happened was that the farmer, no doubt startled at first when that wild-looking outfit dashed up, reflected that not in years, if ever, had a candidate for the state senate come all that way to ask for his vote. The visit made him feel important. As for the young man's dandified appearance, well, he was one of those rich Hyde Park Roosevelts, and how else would a person expect him to dress? Anyhow, young squirt though he might be, a man could see that he was nobody's fool, and he was a hearty, happy sort that knew how to get along with folks. The farmer decided that he rather liked the guy and proved it on election day. Roosevelt swept the district.

As far as the State of New York was concerned, the election of a new state senator in one district didn't mean anything, and even to the active politicians it didn't mean much. The old pros put on their spectacles and took a careful look at the young man, but they didn't get excited. They had seen too many young men get off to a brilliant start, only to peter out in a few months and be forgotten within a year. Roosevelt had run a startling race, and for that reason they looked him over carefully. But what would he do when he got into the senate? Would he vanish into the crowd, or would he show that he had something more than a new and successful way of campaigning? The professionals would wait and see. But they would keep an eye on him.

The importance of this election was not to the public, nor to the politicians, but to the candidate, and not because he had won a seat in the legislature. At last he had found a game he could really play. In football, baseball, tennis, rowing, about the best that could be said of him was "not bad." So had been his performance in law school. So had been his career in law practice. But in this game of politics he had been better than "not bad"; he had been definitely good. More than that, he felt in his bones that with practice he could become a star player, maybe even a champion. From this time on, although he sometimes did other things —law, business, writing books—they were always on the side; his real game was politics. Franklin D. Roosevelt had come to himself.

As the new senator had hoped, 1910 was a Democratic year. The Democrats won Congress. They also elected a governor of New York and a majority of the state legislature, a thing almost unheard of. On account of the way district lines were drawn, the heavy Democratic majority in New York City was outweighed by the small districts upstate in which relatively few Republican votes could elect a member of the legislature.

In addition to the New York governor, the Democrats that year elected twenty-five other governors, one of them, in New Jersey, named Woodrow Wilson. Also in the strangely Democratic legislature sent to Albany that year was another young man beside Roosevelt not soon to be forgotten. A member of the assembly from New York City, his name was Alfred Emmanuel Smith.

Roosevelt knew as well as any old pro that what he had done so far was merely to get through the gate. His performance on the field was what would count. He also knew that the game of politics is a rough one, with few rules and public opinion as the only referee. If he charged into that scrimmage and somebody stepped on his face, he needn't expect any nursing aid from his teammates, to say nothing of the opposition. But he wasn't worried. His campaign for the senate had been rough part of the time, and very hard work all the time. Yet from start to finish he had had a whale of a good time, a far better time than he had ever had attending to routine business in a law office. And he had come out on top.

So when the legislature met and he went to Albany to attend his first session, he meant to stay on top. He didn't intend to vanish in the crowd and let the party leaders forget him.

In New York politics the city has always been the main strength of the Democratic party. The governor, usually, and the legislature, nearly always, were Republicans. In 1910 Charles F. Murphy was the head of Tammany Hall, the Democratic organization, which made him the undisputed Democratic boss of New York City. So when the Democrats unexpectedly elected a governor and a majority of the legislature as well, Murphy assumed that the election made him boss of the whole state.

At that time—and up to 1913—United States Senators were elected by the legislatures, not by the people. A Senator was to be elected in 1910, so Murphy sent word to the Democratic legislators that they were to vote for one of his most faithful followers, William F. Sheehan, nicknamed Blue-eyed Billy. As a matter of fact, there wasn't much against Blue-eyed Billy, except that his election would mean giving Murphy one vote in the Senate in Washington. Sheehan had made a lot of money in the street-railway business, and he had given plenty to the Tammany organization, which is why Murphy was for him; but that practice was the way things went at the time, and few regarded it as buying the seat. In his politics Sheehan was very conservative, which Roosevelt didn't like.

But the real sticker for the upstate men, including Roosevelt, was the idea of jumping through the hoop whenever Charles Murphy snapped his fingers. They flatly wouldn't do so. Eventually, they doped out a scheme for putting the skids under Blue-eyed Billy. He had to have a majority of both houses. The Republicans, of course, were solidly against him, and in the two houses the Democrats had a majority of only about ten. So if more than ten Democrats in each house failed to vote, nobody could be elected.

Roosevelt then made an agreement with eighteen or twenty anti-Murphy men. Each morning, when the legislature met, they took their seats, answered the roll call, and then marched out before a vote for Senator could be taken. The vote showed Sheehan leading, but about ten votes short of a majority. No election.

At first everyone assumed that Boss Murphy would soon wear down the rebels, because he could bring all kinds of pressure to bear on them and he did. He did some pretty mean things, such as finding out where a man owed money and then getting his creditor to demand payment, or taking advertising away from another who owned a country newspaper. But days passed, and then weeks passed, with no election. Franklin, or rather Eleanor, had rented a house in Albany for the session, and to Roosevelt's house the rebels marched every day. There they sat all day and half the night, until the legislature adjourned, swapping stories, playing games, and smoking so many cigars that the smell drove Eleanor and the children up to the third floor. But they would not knuckle under to the boss.

In the end, Murphy had to compromise. He withdrew Blue-eyed Billy and offered instead another of his followers, a respectable old stuffed shirt that the rebels, having made their point, could vote for, which they did. So Murphy got his vote in Washington, but to get it he had the fight of his life. The newspapers, naturally, made much of the story, and all New York State knew that the powerful Boss Murphy had run into one man who wasn't afraid of him and didn't hesitate to stand up to him.

In particular, one newspaper man, Albany representative of the *New York Herald,* was so fascinated that he made himself Roosevelt's press agent and stayed on the job the rest of his life. He was Louis McHenry Howe.

So the Poughkeepsie politicians who undertook to use this young man found themselves used to give him a start in politics; and Boss Murphy, who intended to use him to make an example to other rebels, found himself used to give the man a reputation that extended all over the State of New York and beyond. From the very beginning, using Roosevelt was like playing with dynamite; but most politicians didn't realize so for years.

CHAPTER VIII

# WILSON'S ADMINISTRATION

More than fifty years later it is hard for us to understand why people felt as they did and acted as they did in 1912. When we take up almost any of what they called the great issues of that day they seem so mild and harmless that we wonder why anybody got excited about them.

For instance, the man who was elected governor of New Jersey in 1910 asked the legislature of that state to pass seven new laws, some dealing with business corporations, some with taxes, and some with elections. They were promptly named the Seven Sisters. The fight before they were passed was tremendous, but in the end passed they were. Yet as we look at them now they do not seem terrific. Certainly they were nothing that could upset the whole system of American government, as their opponents said they would.

But the uproar attracted the attention of the whole country, and when the governor, who was a Democrat, won, many Democrats in other states decided that there was a leader who could lead the party all over the country, not merely in New Jersey. One who began to think so was Franklin D. Roosevelt. He took the trouble to go down to Trenton to talk face-to-face with Governor Woodrow Wilson and came away firmly convinced that the Democratic party needed this man. He resolved then and there to do everything he could to persuade New York to vote for Wilson at the Democratic convention in 1912.

From the very first day they met, Franklin Roosevelt admired Woodrow Wilson immensely, but that he ever liked him is doubtful. Wilson was not an easy man to like. True, his immediate family and a few very close friends found him charming, but to the rest of the world he was a bit standoffish. Wilson was a religious man, a strong Presbyterian, who believed right is right and wrong is wrong, and every grown man knows which is which. He admitted that the best of men might be mistaken in trying to tell what is wise and what is unwise, but as between right and wrong, no sir! Every man can know and therefore ought to know the difference, and if he chooses the wrong, the fault is his own.

Nevertheless, Roosevelt's judgment was right. As we see them now the Seven Sisters were not so much, but they meant something important at that time. They meant that the man who had proposed them believed, as Theodore Roosevelt had believed, that control of the country was slipping out of the hands of the people and into the hands of a few rich and powerful men who could be expected to use it to take care of themselves first, and of the people later, if at all. Wilson's course in New Jersey showed that he believed that this situation was all wrong. So did both Roosevelts, and as Franklin was a Democrat, the decision that Wilson was his man was easy for him.

He knew that Boss Murphy, although he called himself a Democrat, could not be expected to support Wilson, for Murphy was another who took care of himself first and was more in sympathy with the rich and powerful than with the mass of the people. But if the New York Democrats outside the city, the upstate Democrats, could be persuaded to support Wilson he would have part of the New York delegates to the convention, and they would be a big help, even though the majority would be Murphy's followers.

So early in 1912 Roosevelt and a handful of other friends of Wilson organized a committee to work for the New Jersey governor in upstate New York. They had some success. Roosevelt was chosen as a delegate to the national convention, which was to meet in Baltimore, and so were a respectable number of other Wilson men. Murphy had more, and he had told them to vote for Champ Clark, a

Missouri Democrat who was Speaker of the House of Representatives; but Wilson had enough to show that some parts of New York State were for him, however the city might go.

That Baltimore convention has never been forgotten, because it was the rowdiest in the history of either of the big parties. The point was that Theodore Roosevelt was raising Cain with the Republican party, threatening to take it away from Taft and the conservatives. If he succeeded, and the Democratic party also went liberal, the conservatives would have nowhere to go, so they made a last-ditch stand at Baltimore to hold one of the major parties if they couldn't take both.

They settled on Champ Clark as their man, and they very nearly put him over. They would have done so except for the old rule, adopted in 1836, that a Democratic nominee must have, not a simple majority, but two thirds of all the convention votes, and Clark could never get two thirds.

The man who broke up the struggle was William J. Bryan, the old liberal candidate in 1896, 1900, and 1908. Some said that, in spite of having been beaten three times, Bryan still wanted the nomination for himself. Maybe he did, but he would do anything rather than see it go to a man favored by Boss Murphy and Tammany. So at a critical moment he got on the platform and made a speech saying that although his Nebraska delegation was pledged to Clark, he, for one, was not going to vote for any candidate of the big-money, Wall Street crowd.

Franklin Roosevelt was in the thick of the convention,

rushing around arguing, urging, pleading with delegates to vote for Wilson. At one moment he very nearly got into a fist fight with a delegate who was holding the New York State banner and would not allow it to be carried in a parade of Wilson men around the hall. Roosevelt tore the banner from his hands and carried it anyhow, while bystanders held off the delegate who wanted to hit him. Of course, at this time he was a very small potato in national politics, but still Wilson's friends noticed that he was there and working hard for Wilson.

Back in New York he continued to work, lining up votes for the election in November and at the same time running himself for reelection to the state senate. But in August bad luck struck. He came down with typhoid fever. It took him out of the campaign at the worst possible moment, and for a time his political career seemed to be finished, once and for all.

It might have been, too, except for Howe. Louis McHenry Howe was nothing much to look at, a little, dried-up, wizened-faced fellow that strangers often made the mistake of dismissing as of no importance. But for years he had been a newspaper reporter covering the legislature and the state capitol, and what he hadn't learned about political dickering and dealing and campaigning simply wasn't worth knowing. When Roosevelt took to his bed, Howe took over his campaign, running it almost entirely by mail and forcing everybody, including Eleanor and Sara, to help.

Fortunately, 1912 was a big Democratic year. Theodore

Roosevelt did split the Republican party after Taft was nominated, forming a party of his own to which he gave the name of Progressive. But he began the campaign by announcing, "I feel as strong as a bull moose," so it was popularly known as the Bull Moose party. He got four million votes, and it is often said that he thereby elected Wilson. However, if he had not been in the race some of his votes would certainly have gone to Wilson and if as many as half had done so, the Democrat would have been elected anyhow. Hence, to say that the Bull Moose elected the Democrat is by no means certainly true.

Be that as it may, Wilson won easily and Franklin, in spite of his illness, scraped through. But the Republicans won the New York legislature so when he returned to Albany, although he was fully recovered from his illness, there was not much that he could do. All winter, therefore, Roosevelt spent most of his time cultivating the friendship of the party leaders he had met at the convention.

Then when the Democratic Day of Jubilee came, and he went down to Washington to attend the inauguration, on March 4, 1913, he was recognized as a young man who had done some good work for Wilson in New York. Thus he was entitled to meet all the party big shots and perhaps might be given a minor job in the administration, for the party needed bright young men. There was talk of an assistant's place in the Treasury Department, and Roosevelt would have taken it, although he had no great liking for figures. Fortunately, it didn't work out.

A little later, however, he met the man whom Wilson

Roosevelt, as Assistant Secretary of the Navy, inspecting the New York Navy Yard in 1913, accompanied by Eleanor

had chosen to be Secretary of the Navy. This man took an instant liking to young Roosevelt, and before their conversation ended he asked, "How would you like to be Assistant Secretary of the Navy?"

This offer was a break indeed! All his life Roosevelt had been crazy about boats and the sea, and he had become a first-rate amateur sailor. Of course, his experience was all with pleasure craft, and he preferred sailboats. But he had always had a lively interest in the Navy and had read every book about it that he could lay his hands on. Probably he knew more already about the history of the Navy than half the admirals did. Then to be next to the top man in the Navy—well, the opportunity was tremendous. To cap everything, this job was the very one that Theodore had held many years before, and the job that had started him on his great career. That precedent made it perfect!

But Roosevelt and his new chief were certainly the most oddly assorted pair in Washington. Josephus Daniels, up to that time, had been the editor-owner of a newspaper in what was then the small city of Raleigh, in North Carolina. For years his political idol had been Bryan and, like Bryan, he prided himself on being one of the plain people and looking the part. He fancied clothes of a rather old-fashioned cut, black string neckties, and slouch hats. He looked for all the world like a country editor come to the big city and sure to be the victim of every slick, smooth-talking swindler he met. The high officers of the Navy were horrified when they had their first look at their new Secretary.

Roosevelt wasn't horrified, he was merely amused; but

at first he was fooled as badly as all the rest. Yet if he had studied the record he might have realized that this apparent simpleton was in reality one of the shrewdest political operators in the country. Josephus Daniels had been on the Democratic National Committee through at least four Presidential campaigns and was its director of publicity part of the time. He had matched wits with the toughest political double-dealers in both parties and had rarely come off second best. Above all, he knew Congress better than any other man not a member except, perhaps, a few veteran reporters who had studied it as long as he, and from the same angle.

Roosevelt with Josephus Daniels (first from left) and President Woodrow Wilson (third from left) at a Washington ceremony in 1913

Nevertheless, this combination of the country bumpkin and the city dude—to put it more politely, the sturdy yeoman and the lordly aristocrat—amused Washington hugely, and the laughter continued for months, Roosevelt joining in at first. But he quit laughing when he began to realize how perfectly they were matched. He was friendly with the admirals, and they found him easy to talk to because he spoke their language. If anyone got out of line however, he could be as hard-boiled as any of them. Daniels let him do most of the talking to the high brass.

But on Capitol Hill Daniels could thread his way swiftly through a political maze in which Roosevelt would have been completely lost. He knew the strength and weakness of every important member, so he knew exactly when to use soothing words and when to turn on the heat. Thus with the Assistant Secretary getting tightened efficiency from the service, and the Secretary getting the money and necessary legislation from Congress, the Navy zoomed.

CHAPTER IX

# WORLD WAR I

For ninety-nine years, from 1815 when the French Emperor, Napoleon I, was defeated to 1914 when the German Emperor, Wilhelm II, got the idea that he was a new Napoleon, there had been no general war in Europe. When any kind of arrangement has lasted for that long most people are sure to think that it is going to last forever. Who is to tell them anything else? The people who know what things were like before have all died, and those who are living have never known anything else. Before 1914 many men who thought themselves, and were thought by others, to be wise had dreamed up arguments to prove that there never could be another general war.

Most Americans believed these arguments, and there is nothing to show that Franklin D. Roosevelt was different from the rest. Clearly, in 1913, he wasn't thinking about Europe, he was thinking about the United States Navy, whose business, as he saw it, was to protect the Americas and the Philippines. Europe could take care of itself and the rest of the world. This belief was a terrible mistake, but it was a mistake of all Americans, not of any one man in particular.

Although historians still do not agree on the reasons why the First World War began, the course of events that led to it proceeded in this way. A group of fanatics from the country then called Serbia, now a part of Yugoslavia, killed Archduke Francis Ferdinand, who was the crown prince of Austria. But Austria, not content with promptly hanging the murderer, insisted that this crime was more than a murder, it was an insult to Austria by Serbia, and stupid Austrian officials decreed that Serbia should be crushed. But Russia had long ago agreed to protect Serbia against Austria, and Germany had agreed to assist Austria in case of trouble with Russia. France had promised Russia her help if she were attacked by Germany, so Germany, to get at France, crashed through Belgium, which Britain had agreed to protect. The British did not go to war to seize the German colonies, nor did the Germans aspire to loot the Bank of England. Everyone was fighting for some idea of national honor and prestige, each calling God to witness how righteous he was.

In 1914 what Roosevelt, a minor official, had to think about was the United States Navy. Regardless of who had started the war, in a matter of time somebody probably would be taking a shot at the United States flag. Roosevelt's job was to see that when that day came the Navy would be able to shoot back, and to hit what it shot at. That ability meant target practice and lots of it. But every shot from a big Naval gun costs much money, and Congress had been skimpy with funds for ammunition. Getting the money was Secretary Daniels' specialty, so the Assistant Secretary didn't worry his head on that score; he spent his time on the ships and the men. The seagoing personnel didn't bother him much. Officers and men seemed up to their job. But the shore installations, drydocks, shipyards, warehousing and stores, and things of that kind had grown slack and inefficient, partly because Congress, for political reasons, insisted on keeping up many installations that were no longer of any real use to the Navy.

One of Roosevelt's first and hardest jobs was tightening up this service so that when a warship put in for supplies or repairs it could get what was needed promptly and could put out to sea again with the least possible delay.

But as the war increased in fury and spread farther and farther across the world, Roosevelt and his chief realized that simply tightening up what existed was not enough. The Navy must be expanded—more ships, more men, more fuel oil, more ammunition, and more up-to-date arms. But this expansion was a delicate matter. President Wilson, bent on keeping out of the war, wanted to do nothing that would look like a threat to either side. He flatly refused to enlarge the Army to any considerable extent. But our merchant ships were already being seized by the Allies and sunk by the Germans, and Wilson admitted that protecting our own ships was a duty we could not avoid, so he was more favorable toward building up the Navy.

At that, Congress took its own time about passing appropriations, so Daniels and Roosevelt, knowing that time was just what we did not have, cut some pretty fine corners. Years later Roosevelt remembered a time when an appropriation for some big guns was slowly creeping through Congress. Roosevelt was pretty sure it would pass, but it hadn't passed when a manufacturer came to him and offered to start making the guns immediately if he could get a contract on which he could borrow money to buy the steel and pay his men until the first guns were delivered. So Roosevelt signed the contract on the spot. It amounted to ninety million dollars, and if Congress hadn't passed that bill the official who signed the contract would have been liable for the whole amount. Roosevelt did not have half of a hundredth part of ninety million dollars, so he said he figured that if things had gone wrong they could have sent him to jail for a hundred years. But the Navy got the guns, which made the risk worthwhile, and Congress finally passed the bill so everything worked out all right.

In 1917 what everybody dreaded happened. Even Wilson

could no longer find a way to stay out of the war; and when he went in, he went in determined, as he told Congress, to use "force without stint or limit."

When we declared war, on April 6, 1917, Roosevelt's first impulse was to rush out and get into a Naval uniform. To sit at a desk, safe in Washington, while other men of his age were fighting, made him ashamed of himself. But when he offered his resignation, Daniels put his foot down; and when Roosevelt was insistent on going to sea, the President put *his* foot down. They could find plenty of young men who could soon learn to do an ensign's job, but what Roosevelt had learned in four years about the intricate business of running the department could not be picked up quickly by anybody else. The President told him flatly that his duty was at that desk, and there he would stay. He wasn't advising him, he was ordering him. And that was that.

At the very end, when plainly the war was won, Wilson relented and told him he could go. But the permission was too late. He never got into any of the fighting.

The shooting war ended at eleven o'clock in the morning of November 11, 1918, but the end of the shooting was the beginning of the war of words that lasted another two years. The United States, like the other countries, had been fighting, not for any material thing, but for an idea. The difference was that the United States was frank about it from the start. We could afford to be, for our idea was one that most of the world approved. So at the beginning the President, speaking for the people, announced that America didn't want to take anybody's land, or money, or

Roosevelt on an inspection trip at the U. S. Naval Air Station, Pauillac, France, 1918

people, and would claim none when the war was won. What America did want, and would make every effort to get, was a system under which the people of every nation might set up any form of government they liked and live under it without interference as long as they did not interfere with their neighbors.

When the people control their own form of government, it is a democracy. Wilson stated flatly that our aim was "to make the world safe for democracy." Everybody on our side said, "Fine!" and even the Germans admitted that the idea was all right. But among the people who held the real power in Europe, almost nobody believed that the intention could be realized. Yet, knowing how badly they needed American help, these rulers were ready to agree to anything, sure that they could wriggle out of the agreement as soon as the war was won.

Wilson had a pretty good notion of what they were thinking, so when the conference to write the peace treaty assembled at Paris, he went there in person to see that our project was written into the treaty. The trip may have been a mistake, because it startled the American people. Except when Theodore Roosevelt went down to take a look while the United States was digging the Panama Canal, no President had gone out of the country while he was in office, and many Americans thought his doing so was unlawful. It wasn't. There had never been a law saying that the President must remain in the country, but Wilson's enemies raised such a clamor that they persuaded many that Wilson had done something dreadful in going to Paris.

But if the trip was a mistake, letting the European rulers cut the heart out of the thing for which we had sacrificed thousands of soldiers and billions of dollars would have been a much worse one. So Wilson went—and ran into a fight that raged for months and completely exhausted him. Since Russia's government had gone to pieces, she was left out, and the fight was Wilson against Georges Clemenceau of France and Vittorio Orlando of Italy, with Lloyd George of England shifting back and forth, and dozens of smaller nations adding to the confusion. These men were known as the Big Four until Orlando, having taken a terrific drubbing, quit in a rage, and they became the Big Three. Wilson lost on many minor points, but he carried the main one. The treaty set up a League of Nations, which was to be the instrument for carrying out the American idea.

But he came back to run into a fight more vicious than the one in Paris. Since 1912 Theodore Roosevelt had been left almost completely out of things, a position that he simply could not stand. As the war ended, his health was failing rapidly, which probably weakened his judgment. At any rate, he developed the notion that all of what he chose to regard as his slights and humiliations were due to the malice of Woodrow Wilson, and he developed a hatred for the man that passed all reasonable bounds. His friend and political ally, Senator Lodge of Massachusetts was the kind of political fanatic who could sincerely believe that only a Republican victory in the next election could save the nation. While Wilson was still in Paris, Lodge sat by what was to be Theodore Roosevelt's deathbed, and they agreed that if the treaty Wilson brought back proved to be a good one—they did not yet know what was in it—he would become such a national hero that the Democrats would certainly win in 1920. So together they concocted a scheme to defeat *any* treaty Wilson might bring back.

The agreement sounds incredible, but Theodore Roosevelt's sister was present, heard the whole thing, and was so far from seeing anything wrong with it that she published it gleefully a few years later.

Theodore died before the big fight began, but Lodge carried the plan through to the letter, and Wilson unfortunately played into his hands in several ways. He, too, as events proved, was a dying man; at the height of the battle in Paris he suffered a stroke, and a second one after his return. Although he lingered until 1924 he was never again an effective force in politics. So his own fellow-citizens destroyed the idea that Wilson had successfully defended against all the potentates of Europe.

All this struggle Franklin D. Roosevelt watched at close range. Not being a member of either the Senate or the Cabinet, he had no prominent part in the fight, but he saw it all and remembered what he saw. It was the sharpest kind of lesson in practical politics, and it helped him a great deal in later years.

The collapse of the President, followed by the rejection of the League of Nations, threw the Democratic party into confusion and dismay. It also threw Europe into confusion and dismay, but most Americans paid small attention to that problem. Up to 1914 they had known little and cared less about Europe, except as a place for summer tourists to visit.

It soon became clear that all the Great War had done was to upset the Balance of Power without putting anything else in its place. This development wasn't making the world safe for democracy. On the contrary, it was making it unsafe for any and every system, democracy included. Americans felt that somewhere, somehow, they had been double-crossed. Some blamed Wilson, some blamed Lodge, some blamed our allies, some blamed the new Russian government, then called Bolshevik, later Communist. The situation was all very confusing, and, as usually happens, millions took out their bewilderment on the party in power.

By the time the nominating conventions assembled in the summer of 1920, neutral observers were saying that no

Democrat would have a ghost of a chance at the election in November. This prediction chilled the ambition of all the really big Democrats. Who wants to run when he is practically certain to take a licking? They suddenly became modest, each insisting that someone else would be a better choice. The truth was that each knew that one bad beating can ruin a big political reputation. The delegates finally chose James M. Cox, who had no big reputation, although he had been a very good governor of Ohio.

The second place was even less desirable, so when the name of Franklin D. Roosevelt was suggested it seemed ideal. Firstly, the name impressed many people who still remembered Theodore. Secondly, everyone admitted that the Navy had been well run during the war, and some of the credit certainly belonged to the Assistant Secretary. Thirdly, he had no big political reputation to be damaged by a possible defeat, and he was eager to run. So they nominated him for Vice-President, not expecting much from him but needing to nominate somebody.

Despite everything, Cox and Roosevelt put up a good fight. The size of the popular vote was immense, because women voted for the first time, and so the winner's majority was immense. But the Democrats held 127 electoral votes, which was enough to keep them as a real opposition party. Furthermore, the candidate for Vice-President came out of the campaign as a real national figure. He worked hard throughout, making speeches all over the country and speaking well. What was more important, to him, he met party leaders of all types and made a good impression on

Roosevelt accepting nomination for the Vice-Presidency,
Hyde Park, New York, August 9, 1920

Roosevelt with Governor James M. Cox
on a Presidential campaign trip, 1920

them. He listened, as well as talked, and did his best to size them up, something that he liked to do and that came naturally to him. He made notes constantly and ended the campaign with a vast fund of information about the men who actually got out the vote on election day. All of which he filed for future reference.

But the Democrats were beaten, and Roosevelt was out of office, if not out of politics. He had failed to make Theodore's second job, the Vice-Presidency, so he turned back to the law, because there was nothing else to do. Still, he was not hopelessly depressed. At any rate, the whole Democratic party now knew that he was alive, and he did not doubt that the party's time would come; and when it did he would be right on the spot.

CHAPTER X

# PARALYSIS

In 1920 Franklin Roosevelt was thirty-eight years old. His life was a little more than half over. He was no longer a boy, he was a full-grown man with a wife and family; yet for high politics, top-level politics, he was still rather young. A man who has been nominated for Vice-President at thirty-eight has made a national reputation pretty fast. Fifty is closer to the average age for an office that big.

At this time he was what we call a well-educated man, both in book learning and in knowing how to deal with people. Yet the flat truth is that in 1920 at the age of thirty-eight, Franklin D. Roosevelt did not amount to much.

Oh, he was not a failure—far from it. If he had remained just what he was then—except growing more so as he grew older—when he died people would have called him a successful man, perhaps even an eminent man. Very likely he would have been a Cabinet officer, or an ambassador, and certainly a leader of the Democratic party. One can believe that he might have been a President and done as well in the White House as he did on the tennis court—that is to say, not bad, but not very good, either. He would have been compared with such Presidents as Monroe and Polk and Cleveland, but never with Jefferson or Lincoln.

The fact is that Roosevelt, up to this time, had had things too easy to be forced to extend himself. True, he had taken his bumps. During the war he tried to become a senator from New York, and a smaller man, James W. Girard, beat him easily. Then he had run for Vice-President and had been beaten again. But these blows were not really hard ones. They stung a bit, but they were not the kind that takes all the fight out of a man and leaves him permanently whipped. They taught him not to lead with his chin, and he bounced back fast.

There was something else that these slams had failed to knock out of Roosevelt. His friends hate to admit this fault, but even as late as 1920 he was a bit of a snob. Of course, his snobbery wasn't the cheap sort that makes some people bow and scrape before the rich and well-known even if they have neither brains nor character. Roosevelt had too much sense to make himself ridiculous in that way. But he did have a slight touch of the feeling that his class was a little above the masses of the people, and he was still too much inclined to judge by appearances. This inclination was the thing that made him give Frances Perkins the brush-off when she first tried to get him to help her program of social work, and that made him laugh at Josephus Daniels' string tie and broad-toed shoes. To be sure, he was smart enough to learn soon that these people were able and valuable. But as late as 1920 there was a touch of the hoity-toity in him. It'was not enough to prevent him from being an able man, but it might have prevented him from being a great one.

For at this time Franklin D. Roosevelt, with all his education, had not yet learned the hardest lesson of all. He did not yet know what makes a man not merely good but a champion in any walk of life. In sports, in business, in politics, in war, in peace, in anything, the champion is the fighter who can be beaten to a pulp, cut up, bloodied, and finally knocked flat, but who can yet get up and fight again. One doesn't learn that ability by hearing about it. One learns it when one needs it, and thus far Franklin D. Roosevelt had never needed it. But he was about to.

By election day in November, 1920, he was tuckered out. He had traveled thousands of miles, he had made hundreds of speeches, he had shaken hands with more people than anybody could count. In the time between he had worked hard at party headquarters. He was all in.

Then when the election was over and lost, he needed to find some other occupation, which meant arranging a new law partnership, setting up offices, and looking for clients.

This work was not too hard, for the campaign had given him a national reputation, and plenty of lawyers were glad to have such a celebrity as a partner. Still, his affairs took a lot of arranging, and what with his personal concerns and helping the Democratic party leaders pick up the pieces after the shattering defeat, he was busy all winter. So when the summer of 1921 came, and pressure slacked off a bit, he was very glad indeed to get away to Campobello to sail and fish and swim and be with the family away from politics and business.

One day when he and the boys had been out sailing, as they came back to the mooring they noticed smoke rising among the trees not far from their camp and feared it was a forest fire starting. So they rushed over to fight it. After an hour or so they beat it out, but they came back to the camp grimy with sweat and smoke and dust, so they took a swim to wash off. Even in midsummer the sea-water around Campobello Island is so cold that most people call it icy, but the Roosevelts were used to it and didn't mind. When they walked up to the house afterward, they found that the mail had arrived and Franklin sat down in his wet bathing suit and read a number of letters. The doctors think that what with being tired to begin with, then fighting the fire, then plunging into cold water, and then sitting in a wet suit, he gave his system such a shock that it could not resist a virus that he had picked up somewhere.

Anyhow, that night he was taken very ill. Local doctors decided that he had flu—then called grippe or Spanish influenza—and treated him for that condition. But he got worse and began to suffer dreadful pain. After three days specialists, called in from Boston, discovered that it was something far worse than flu, it was the disease, then considered dreadful, called infantile paralysis, because more children than grown people caught it. The scientific name is poliomyelitis, which people usually shorten to polio. At this time the famous Doctor Salk—and later Doctor Sabin—had not yet discovered how to prevent, or at least to help, polio. In 1921 it was regarded as often deadly, and always incurable. For several days Roosevelt seemed to be dying, and when they finally pulled him through alive, his legs were paralyzed. Apparently he would spend the rest of his life in bed, or at best in a wheelchair, although some polio victims, with the aid of steel braces on their legs, had learned to walk a little.

Now the world assumed that Roosevelt was down for the count. He might live a long time, but only as a helpless invalid, not as anybody who could play an important part in anything, least of all in the rough-and-tumble world of politics. There were black moments when he feared that the world was right, and if he had ever really believed so, he would have been finished. But he never quite did. Always he had somewhere within him the determination to get up and fight again. Two reasons why he never quite broke were Eleanor and Louis Howe. Even Sara gave up. She protested when Eleanor and Louis kept bringing to the sickroom news of what was going on in the world, asking

Franklin's advice about things, especially problems of politics, and writing scores and hundreds of letters for him to political leaders all over the country.

Sara thought they were worrying the sick man uselessly. She believed that the sooner he became reconciled to life in a wheelchair, and quit thinking about anything beyond his own four walls, the better life would be for him. But Eleanor and Louis believed that protection of that kind would be the way to kill him in short order or, if it didn't kill him, to reduce him to a worthless thing of no value to himself or anyone else.

So they did everything they could to fan his spark of determination into flame. They brought him all the news. They argued with him over everything that the newspapers reported. They reminded him incessantly that his brain hadn't been touched, only his legs. They pointed out that he had never been an acrobat, that he had always depended on his head, not his legs, and that his head was as good as ever. As soon as the acute part of the illness had passed and the pain had gone, they brought visitors to see him, especially people important in the political world, and they encouraged arguments and discussions and plans for bringing back the Democratic party from its low ebb. They nearly drove Sara out of her mind, but they put spirit into the sick man at the moment when he needed it most. Incidentally Eleanor, once the shy wallflower, learned more about the inside workings of American politics, because of her incessant letter-writing and consultations, than most women ever dream exists.

She and Louis Howe did not make Franklin Roosevelt the man he became. He did so himself. But as the seconds of a battered prizefighter sponge his face and knead his muscles and yell at him that he is doing fine, until they get their man on his feet, so these two labored over the man they were backing in the political ring. And when the gong rang, he came out fighting.

Franklin D. Roosevelt never came anywhere close to despair again. He spoke of those days lightly. He once told a friend that when he had spent two years in bed trying desperately to wiggle his big toe and finally succeeded, he would never again believe that anything is impossible. The fact is that he felt that the worst had already happened, and anything that might come later would be less serious. When a man has endured dreadful pain and has looked death straight in the face, but has come out alive, what else is there that can scare him? One who can whip pain and death will take on anything else and laugh about it; and others, looking on, will begin to suspect that he is unbeatable. Up to this time Roosevelt, as a politician, had been not bad, maybe even a bit of a star. But it was while he was flat on his back in a hospital bed that he became a champion.

CHAPTER XI

# THE HAPPY WARRIOR

Polio is one of those diseases that are soon over, as far as the violent sickness is concerned, but often leave damage that cannot be repaired. Roosevelt had it in 1921, and by 1923 his general health was as good as ever, but his legs were left so weak that he could hardly use them at all. Still, he kept trying. At first he could move about only in a wheelchair. Then the family got him a walker, a steel frame on wheels so made that he could support his weight on his arms and hands and push himself about. Finally, he acquired a set of steel braces, which he could fit on his legs to stiffen them.

With their help, he could stand and even walk a little. At last he got to the stage where, with a pair of sticks and a helping arm, he could walk, even up a ramp. But he never could climb stairs.

Yet Eleanor and Louis Howe were speaking the truth when they kept telling him that his head was all right. Many people believe that his brain was more than all right, that it was better than ever, because during those months in bed, and in a wheelchair, he had been using it constantly to do a great deal of hard thinking.

One way in which the doctors told him he might get back some strength in his legs was by swimming, because while swimming the water would carry most of his weight so that weak muscles could move his legs. So Roosevelt spent a great deal of time in a swimming pool, with the result that his chest and arms grew large and powerful. In the end he was, from the waist up, an uncommonly strong man.

Of course, a man's brain doesn't grow bigger, as his arms do, by constant exercise, but there is no doubt that it grows stronger by constant thinking. Certainly when Roosevelt got back into an office he could think fast and straight, and those who knew him both before and after his illness—Louis Howe, for one—believed that he thought faster and straighter afterward than he had ever done before.

That is as it may be, but this much is certain: when he began again to take part in business affairs, his mind moved with a speed that astonished those with whom he dealt. One man who noticed this quality was another lover of ships and the sea. He was a Baltimore businessman whose company had a branch office in New York. His name was Van Lear Black, and he is usually described as a banker, but his New York office wasn't the usual kind of bank. It was a surety business, which is to say, it stood bond for contractors and other businessmen engaged in projects where a failure to make good would cost the other party a lot of money. For a fee, the bonding company agrees to make good if the bonded party doesn't.

To succeed in this kind of business, one must judge, first, the project, and then the people. Sometimes things that are nobody's fault can delay or ruin a job—tornadoes, fires, accidental explosions, things like that. But the chance of such a happening is not great, and a skilled mathematician can figure it to the last decimal point, so the bonding company can make its fee large enough to cover that small chance. But the company must also know the people it deals with so as never to write a bond for a contractor who is crooked, or just no good.

Roosevelt knew nothing about figuring chances, but he knew a great deal about judging people, and for that ability Black offered him a job in his surety office. In later years Roosevelt's enemies said the position wasn't really a job, it was charity, offered because Black was sorry for the crippled man. Such people didn't know Van Lear Black. He was a friend of Roosevelt and he was a generous man, but he didn't run his business on friendship. If Roosevelt had been completely without money, Black might have given him a pension, but he would never have made him an officer of the company. He took that step because he knew Roosevelt would bring in business, and because the new man was acquainted with so many people, of so many types, in so many parts of the country, that his connections would be sound business on which the company would make a profit.

It is true also, that Black was interested in a vast number of things besides banking—aviation, yachting, horse-racing, circuses, and he had a large interest in a newspaper, the *Baltimore Sun*—so he liked a lively fellow who was always starting something, no matter what his line. If Roosevelt's presence brought into the offices of the company a procession of high-ranking politicians, the development was all right with Black. It was both good for business and entertaining. Black was pleased on both counts.

Then when the Presidential election of 1924 was approaching, Black didn't object to Roosevelt's taking part in it. In fact, Black helped out a bit by bringing in people with information to report to Roosevelt what they knew about any political situation. In the end the company gave Roosevelt a leave of absence, and he gave all his time to the campaign.

That political campaign was one of the strangest in American history for, as events turned out, nobody in either party knew what he was doing. Nor were the politicians the only ones who were badly mixed up. The voters were in the same condition, maybe even worse.

The fact is that the people, except a very few men who were wise and farsighted beyond the average, were just beginning to learn that the real problem facing the United States, and the rest of the world, too, was how to clean up the mess left by the great war of 1914 to 1918, which we now call the First World War. The man chosen for President that year should have been the man who knew most about the mess and how to clean it up.

That need is perfectly clear to us now, but it wasn't clear then. Most people thought that cleaning up the war wreckage was a fairly simple job, and that the really big issues were two that had nothing to do with the war. They were religion and racism.

Roosevelt knew that this thinking was all wrong, but what could he do about it? If the voters refused to consider anything but race and religion, he would have to argue about race and religion, even though he was sure we should be thinking about other things. One reason why he couldn't persuade the people to think about the real problem of the economic damage caused by the war was the fact that he did not himself realize how big that problem was. He may have known as much about it as anybody else, but nobody knew much, because the world had never faced exactly that kind of breakdown in international trade before.

What Roosevelt did know, and thought should be of most interest to the people, was that the Republican party had made a dreadful mistake in 1920 when it elected Warren G. Harding President of the United States. The man was not crooked, but he simply wasn't big enough for the job. A smart crook could put over almost anything on him, and many did. The worst that was uncovered was the incident in which certain oil companies were given leases on Western oil lands—Teapot Dome and Elk Hills—that the Navy had been keeping to ensure itself fuel oil in case of another war. This scandal the Democrats thought was enough to win the election for them and so it would have been in ordinary circumstances, but the circumstances were not ordinary.

For one thing, the Democrats didn't discover until 1929 that the companies had paid Secretary of the Interior Albert B. Fall a bribe of $100,000 to sign those leases. In that year Fall went to jail. For another thing, President Harding had died in 1923, and Calvin Coolidge, the Vice-President, had become President. Nobody thought that Coolidge had had anything to do with Teapot Dome so the Republicans nominated him for a full term. Thus the issue of bribery and corruption was partly washed out.

Much more important was the fact that the Democrat's best candidate was the man who was then governor of New York. He was that same Alfred Emmanuel Smith, whom Roosevelt had first met as a member of the legislature in 1910. At that time Al Smith was a Tammany man and Charles Murphy's leader in the assembly, where he dutifully voted for Blue-eyed Billy Sheehan; but he was secretly delighted when Roosevelt led the rebellion that beat Sheehan. The two became great friends, for Roosevelt knew that Smith was honest, even if he did play along with the boss.

In the fourteen years that followed Al Smith rose steadily in politics and in Roosevelt's estimation. At last he was elected governor and proved to be one of the best that the

State of New York had ever had. During his administration Roosevelt did everything he could for Al, and they became political allies.

They were an oddly assorted pair. Except in honesty and brains, Al Smith was everything that Franklin Roosevelt was not. Al had come up the hard way. He was the son of poor Irish immigrants, who never made much money. He grew up almost in the shadow of the Brooklyn Bridge in what was, if not quite a slum, yet a poor district. He went to public schools and never saw the inside of a college. As soon as he was old enough, he quit school and got a job in the Fulton Fish Market. But he was a gay, good-humored fellow and a great favorite at parties, where he could do a song-and-dance act almost good enough for the professional stage. Soon the local bosses discovered that he was a born leader and began to use him in small jobs, then in bigger and bigger ones for the party. Every time he took a step up he learned the new job thoroughly, for even if he lacked schooling he had a fine mind and learned quickly. He had a great deal of common sense, which enabled him to explain complex issues to the voters as well as any politician in New York, and a great deal better than most. He was hugely popular, and well deserved to be.

But in religion he was a Roman Catholic, and at that time there still lingered some of the bitterness left from the period, centuries earlier, when Protestant and Catholic alike considered religion a part of politics. A man who belonged to the other church was certainly an enemy and probably a traitor. The wars of religion that had almost turned Europe into a desert were still remembered. The British, the Dutch, and the Swedes who came to America in the early days were Protestants, and so were the French Huguenots. The Irish were the first Catholics who came in large numbers, and at first they were regarded with

Roosevelt with Governor Alfred E. Smith at a luncheon for Democratic party leaders, Hampton Bays, Long Island, July, 1931

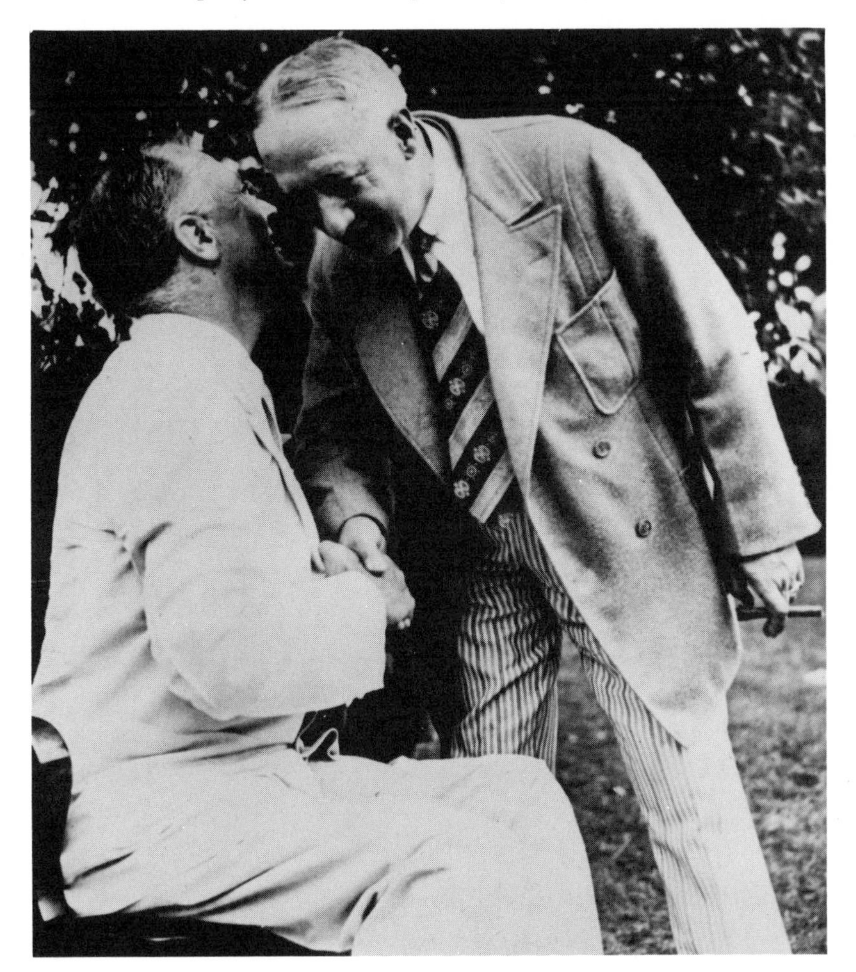

suspicion and hostility. The country had never elected a Catholic President.

To Roosevelt, Smith's religion had nothing to do with the case. It had not prevented him from being a good governor, so why should it prevent him from being a good President? But to many people—more than Roosevelt realized—it meant a great deal, because they still looked on the Roman Church as what it had been three hundred years earlier. Some Protestants who were well aware of how greatly their own religion had altered since it hanged old women for witches at Salem in 1692 would not admit that Catholicism, too, had been casting off bigotry. They thought of Al Smith pretty much as they thought of Phillip II of Spain, who sent the Armada against England in 1688. These fears were silly, but they were real, and Smith and his friends made a mistake when they refused to believe that they were real.

Some years earlier, in 1915, a fanatical old doctor in Georgia had founded a secret society that in the beginning was not very different from a dozen harmless fraternal orders. It imitated the ritual and insignia of the Ku Klux Klan, a genuine terrorist band that operated against Negroes right after the Civil War in 1866. For nearly ten years the new Ku Klux Klan remained small and was hardly heard of outside of Georgia. But then it came under the control of very smart, but very unscrupulous organizers, who saw it as a way of making money and who spread it far beyond the South. At one time the Klan was especially strong in Indiana and Oregon. The society supplied the ignorant and thoughtless with something they very much desired, a scapegoat on whom they could blame all their troubles. The scapegoat was anyone unlike the majority of Georgians, who were native, white, and Protestant. The most numerous classes of such people were Catholics, Negroes, and Jews, although any immigrant, even if he were white and Protestant, was suspected by the Ku Klux Klan.

The Klan was founded on hate, and it preached hatred, with terrible results. Wherever it spread Catholics, Negroes, and Jews were subjected to insults and injuries. Naturally, this outfit hated Al Smith bitterly, and, naturally, Smith's friends, including Roosevelt, were determined not to let the Klan get control of the Democratic party. Therefore, at the convention of 1924, which met in New York, they introduced a resolution denouncing the Klan by name.

It ran into furious opposition, for several reasons. In the first place, Klan votes had elected a great many of the delegates, especially among those from the South and West. At that time the Klan was believed to have about five million members. In the second place, the full extent of the Klan's evil was not yet known. Even as prominent a leader as William Jennings Bryan still held it to be another fraternal order, a little extreme no doubt, but not enough of a danger to justify the Democratic party in denouncing it. Furthermore, Bryan, and many others of the old progressive crowd in the West and South, were deeply suspicious of anything that came out of New York. Many people believe, too, that Bryan, a Presbyterian and a very pious man, was fearful of making a Catholic President. At any rate, he led the fight against the resolution, and it was defeated by a margin of one vote.

Bryan's candidate for the nomination was William G. McAdoo, who had been Secretary of the Treasury under Woodrow Wilson and who was a very able man. But after the defeat of their resolution, the Smith men felt that to nominate McAdoo would amount to making the Democratic party the Ku Klux party, and that they were not going to do. So the fight became bitter to the last degree.

Roosevelt nominated Smith in one of the finest speeches he ever made in his life. After reciting a long list of Smith's battles for the people against those who tried to oppress them, he ended with a quotation from a poem by William Wordsworth:

> This is the happy Warrior. This is he
> That every man in arms should wish to be.

and from that time on his friends delighted in calling Smith the Happy Warrior.

But the eloquence was no use. When the first ballot was taken, nobody had anything near a two-thirds majority. Nor on the second. Nor on the third. Each ballot took an hour or so, even when there was no squabble over some delegate's trying to change half a vote and the others protesting. The convention adjourned to the next day. No majority on the fourth ballot, or on the fifth or the sixth. So it went, day after day. The weather was extremely hot. The delegates grew more and more tired, and the more tired they became the angrier they became. Finally, when the whole crowd

Roosevelt with John W. Davis at Hyde Park on August 7, 1924

was exhausted, both sides gave up, and on the one hundred and third ballot the party nominated John W. Davis, a highly respectable lawyer, but one whom many of the delegates had never heard of and whom nobody wanted.

The country didn't want him either. On election day many Democrats, both Smith men and McAdoo men, stayed at home, and Coolidge, the Republican, won easily, in spite of the Teapot Dome and all the other scandals.

CHAPTER XII

# BACK IN POLITICS

Roosevelt was disappointed, but he wasn't really surprised by the results of the election. After that fight in the convention over the Ku Klux Klan, he knew that the machinery of the Democratic party was a wreck. The old regulars would go through the motions, but not one in ten would really put his back into the campaign, and parties don't win elections that way.

The sad part of the defeat was that Davis really stood for something vastly more important than any of the issues over which his party had torn itself to pieces. He was more than merely a good lawyer. He was a student of government and especially of foreign relations, and he knew that trouble was coming unless we paid more attention to what was going on in Europe and the rest of the world. Perhaps if he had been elected he couldn't have done any more about the international problems than Coolidge did, but at least he knew where the danger lay, and he might have persuaded the country to face it.

Nevertheless, after the election he was out, and in Roosevelt's opinion the first thing that had to be done was to pull the party together again so that it could at least put up a respectable fight in 1928. That job was his public duty. His private duty was to get his legs to working again, if possible. So to these two things he determined to devote himself for the next four years.

The first job he undertook to do by mail. By this time he knew nearly every important Democrat in every state in the Union, and the few he didn't know, Louis Howe did. So between them they began to send out letters in numbers almost beyond belief. The first letter didn't offer advice. It simply asked the leader what shape the party was in in his neighborhood. In some cases the man's neighborhood was a single city or county; in other cases it was a whole state. The letter went on to ask if the party was in bad shape, what did the man think should be done to better it?

Most of the leaders answered, many at great length. As the replies came in Roosevelt and Howe studied them and nearly always they were able to come up with some idea that might work in that particular place. Not all of the ideas were good ones, but at least they were interesting, and some of them were very good indeed. The correspondence became enormous.

There were two results. In the first place, many local leaders who had been stunned by the defeat came to life again and began to think seriously about pulling things together in their locality. So the party began to build up again from the bottom. In the second place, most of the local men were pleased to find somebody at national headquarters interested in their local problems and willing to help. This man Roosevelt seemed to be a live wire, and the Democratic party certainly needed one. As letters went back and forth they became certain of his ability. Roosevelt was slowly building up a great personal following in the party.

The second job, recovering the use of his legs, didn't go so well. Having learned much more about polio than was then known, we know now that recovery was impossible, but Roosevelt kept hoping and did, in fact, make a little progress. Someone told him about a place in Georgia where polio victims had been much benefited by swimming in a pool fed by water from warm springs. So he went there.

It was nothing fancy, but he liked it. Many years earlier Warm Springs had been a popular health resort, but it was pretty badly run down when Roosevelt discovered it. Still, a few cottages were there at least in good enough shape to keep out the rain, the springs were as strong as ever, and the pool could be used. Roosevelt made up his mind that constant swimming in the warm water was doing his legs good, and perhaps they were improving a little. At any rate, the exercise was healthy, and it certainly did his arms and shoulders good. A few years later a stranger, seeing him sitting at his desk with his legs out of sight and only his barrel chest and muscular arms in view, might easily have believed that this husky could pick up an average-size man and throw him downstairs.

At Warm Springs Roosevelt felt fine. For one thing, not many people made the long trip down there to argue with him about business or politics. If anyone did come, he had something important to say. Roosevelt always took a secretary with him, and he wrote and received a large number of letters, so he kept in touch with things, yet he felt that he was relaxing. Not surprisingly, he spent as much time as he could at Warm Springs.

There was another thing about the place to which writers have not paid much attention, although it may have been more important than outsiders have realized in making Roosevelt the kind of man he was. This fact is that other victims of polio were there, and when word got out that Roosevelt liked Warm Springs, the number rapidly increased. Always a friendly soul, he talked to them, high and low, ignorant and learned, children and old people. Many of them were, of course, in very low spirits, and he tried to cheer them up. He organized parties for them, and often in the evening he sat with a crowd around a campfire, singing and telling stories before bedtime.

Without doubt this experience made him realize as he never had before how very many people had gone through all that he had suffered, many of them too poor to afford the doctors and nurses and expensive equipment—braces, wheelchairs, and other things of the kind—that had helped him through the worst days. He never talked much about their troubles, but he felt them very keenly. We know that he did because of his actions.

When he first went there, Warm Springs lacked a great many things that a polio victim needs. To begin with, the pool itself needed fixing up, and doing the job properly meant spending a lot of money. More doctors were needed, more nurses, and more physiotherapists, that is, people especially skilled in treating muscles and nerves damaged by such a disease as polio. Drugs are not much help in such cases, but sometimes massage, special exercises, electric treatment, and appliances such as braces will work wonders. But these things cost much money, and few people who came to Warm Springs had that much.

Although Roosevelt himself didn't have nearly as much as the place needed, he had a lot of rich friends and he went to work on them. They responded as he knew they would, but the time was pressing. Warm Springs was losing money, and in the winter of 1925 and 1926 the people running it came to the end of their rope. They had to get out, so Roosevelt bought it. It cost him something over $200,000, two thirds of what his father had left him. He then established the Georgia Warm Springs Foundation, promising to sell the property to the foundation for what it had cost him. However, if the Foundation had not been able to raise any money, he would have been stuck.

The gamble turned out all right. In a year or two the Foundation raised much more than $200,000, so Roosevelt got his money back, except for $18,000, which was his contribution. He therefore never claimed to be a great benefactor. But he took the risk, which wasn't like him. Never before had he risked two thirds of all he had on one deal, and he never took such a risk again. So he must have felt very keenly the misery of the people who came to Warm Springs.

Perhaps Roosevelt learned nothing at Warm Springs that he hadn't known before with the top of his mind, but there he apparently learned to feel it with his heart. At any rate, he developed a remarkable understanding of how many men take a terrible beating through no fault of their own. He felt more strongly than most political leaders that people crippled not by their own misconduct, but by sheer bad luck, have a right to be helped by those lucky enough to have escaped. He did not regard such help as charity. He thought it was simple fairness. Probably Roosevelt learned to think that way at Warm Springs.

For the rest, he regarded himself as on the sidelines in politics, following the game with interest, but not playing. There he intended to stay until he had recovered the use of his legs, and even Louis Howe thought he was smart to do so. Roosevelt intended to sit out the election of 1928, hoping to make a comeback in 1932.

But the decision was not left to him. He did consent to go to the Democratic convention, meeting in Houston, Texas, and to present the name of Alfred E. Smith again.

This time there was no uproar. For one thing, Bryan was dead and the work of the Ku Klux Klan had been shockingly exposed, first in Louisiana by the *Baltimore Sun,* later in other parts of the country by the *New York World.* By then most of the honest members who had been fooled into joining it had pulled out. For another thing, the country was prosperous, and the Republicans claimed that they had made it so. For a third thing, the Republicans had nominated the very popular Secretary of Commerce, Herbert Hoover, and he would be hard to beat.

So the old pros in the Democratic party, even in the South and West were inclined to say, if Al Smith still wants the nomination, by all means let him have it. It's no good, anyhow, and if it's proved he can't win, maybe we'll be rid of him. So the opposition put up no more than a token resistance, and Smith was nominated on the first ballot. Roosevelt went back to Warm Springs feeling sure, and assured by others including Smith, that he had done his part and, except maybe for making a speech or two, could spend the rest of the year trying to mend his legs and raising money for the Foundation.

But this plan was not to be. Smith's campaign started badly and kept going worse. By October 1, when the New York State Democratic convention met to nominate a candidate for governor, politicians began to doubt that Smith would carry his own state, and without New York he would not have a chance. They believed that Al would hold the city, so the obvious move was to nominate for governor a Democrat strong in upstate New York, and there was only one man who was anything like strong enough—Franklin D. Roosevelt.

He did his best to duck. When they began telephoning from New York the night before the convention, he left Warm Springs to attend a political rally some miles away. But when he returned, Al Smith himself was on the telephone asking him to run as a matter of personal friendship. So, against his better judgment, against the wishes of Eleanor, and against the almost frantic advice of Louis Howe, he consented.

Having decided to go in, Roosevelt went headlong. He launched a campaign as furious as the one that had startled the Dutchess County politicians back in 1910. To his own surprise, he found that he enjoyed it. Back in the game that he loved, and playing now in championship form, he flourished under the strain instead of breaking down. He wound up the campaign with a bang, and he jokingly told friends that if he could spend twelve months campaigning he would be able to throw away the canes that helped him walk.

The returns were a bigger bang. Smith lost New York by 100,000 votes, but Roosevelt carried the state by 25,000.

The outcome was unbelievable. All over the country politicians were stunned. Al Smith unfortunately, was embittered. He didn't understand that without Roosevelt he would have lost the state by half a million, and he felt that somehow his friend had sold him out, although he couldn't say how. Nevertheless, others didn't see the election that way.

CHAPTER XIII

# THE GREAT DEPRESSION

Every new governor when he is inaugurated swears the same oath in the same kind of ceremony and afterward fills the same offices, usually with the same kind of people, except that some are called Republicans and others Democrats. When the legislature assembles, he makes the same kind of speech to the members and presents the same kind of program, that is, a list of laws he advises them to pass. All these things Roosevelt did in the usual way. Even his legislative program was the same kind that Governor Smith had presented. A number of items in it were intended merely to continue what Smith had started, and the new items were of a kind that Smith approved. Smith had been a very good governor indeed, and for eight months or so Roosevelt appeared to be another of the same kind.

But then the roof fell in. The actual tiles covering the capitol in Albany didn't crash, but the stock market in New York City did. The effect was more terrific than if the beams and rafters of a building had given away. The great panic of 1929 struck in October and plunged this country into the great depression out of which it took us ten years to climb.

At the time nobody knew quite what had happened, Governor Roosevelt no more than the next man. After nearly forty years we can see that the real cause was that the destruction of the First World War had finally caught up with Europe and the United States. For ten years Americans had been kidding themselves into believing that Europe could fight for four years and the United States for two, killing ten million men and destroying billions of dollars' worth of property, and then go back to doing business as usual under the same old system. Americans had been covering up, passing the buck, juggling the debt from right hand to left and back again. During the war the United States had lent four billion dollars to the Allies, and after the armistice private citizens lent ten billions more to various countries of Europe, sure that the money would be paid because the old world trading system said that it would. But Europe had burned up the money in the war, and it was gone—gone from America to Europe, and gone from Europe into nowhere.

For ten years the policy of pouring goods into Europe on the theory that we would be paid for them had kept American factories running, American workers busy, and the price of stocks steadily rising. This situation was the prosperity of which the Republicans had boasted in the campaign of 1928. Coolidge, and then Hoover, kept assuring the country that everything was all right, that these conditions could go on forever, so the stock market kept rising.

But when the big lenders realized that they weren't going to be paid, because they couldn't be paid, they went bankrupt. Then the people who had been doing business with them went bankrupt, and failures occurred all down the line. No doubt the government should have paid off the big lenders out of tax money, thus spreading the loss over the whole country pretty evenly. But under the old system that policy would have been regarded as plain stealing, and it might have caused a revolution. So we went on believing what was not so, and in the end the lie backfired on everybody.

When the panic of 1929 suddenly wiped out the whole value of many stocks and sharply reduced the value of others, a great number of people who had thought themselves rich, or at least well-off, found themselves with much less than they had thought they had, or with nothing at all. By millions they quit buying anything except what they had to have to stay alive. This drop in spending threw the stores into trouble, and they quit ordering and discharged clerks. When orders stopped the factories shut down, and factory workers had no job.

Here was exactly the kind of thing Roosevelt had seen at Warm Springs, only ten thousand times bigger. These people had done no wrong any more than had the polio victims at Warm Springs. Yet even as the polio victims were being punished by pain and helplessness, so the unemployed were being punished by hunger and cold because of forces they could not control or even understand. Roosevelt felt that all who escaped had the duty to help those who had not. That is to say, the whole State of New York owed help to the jobless.

President Hoover was facing the same problem with the difference that he had forty-eight states on his hands, while Roosevelt had only one, although it was the biggest of the forty-eight. Hoover no doubt was as horrified as Roosevelt by the misery of the unlucky, and he recognized his duty to do something about it. However, he felt that he had to follow the old rules, which held—although no law said so—that the Federal government cannot deal with a citizen, even to help him. Hoover, therefore, set up an agency called the Reconstruction Finance Corporation, which was allowed to lend government money to factory owners, usually large corporations, to enable them to start their factories again and so supply jobs. But a catch soon appeared in this plan. Many factory owners used the money, not to start their idle machines again, but to pay back money they had previously borrowed from the banks. This development was fine for the banks, but it left the jobless without jobs, still hungry and cold. Yet Hoover felt that he could do no more.

Roosevelt's idea was that at such a time the only rule that counted was the rule that a man who can and will work must be given a paying job by which he can support himself and his family. If private enterprise can't do so, the government, state or Federal, must, and if that procedure is against the rules, so much the worse for the rules. He would do so anyhow. The conservatives screamed that his policy was socialism, but Roosevelt paid no heed. He used all the state money he could lay hands on to create jobs for the unemployed.

However, the task was too big for one state, even New

Campaign headquarters, Buffalo, New York, October, 1930

York, to handle, and things got steadily worse. Still, the people saw that the governor was doing his best, and when he came up for reelection in 1930—the term of a governor of New York was only two years then—he won by a majority of 725,000, a figure that not even Al Smith had ever reached.

Incidentally, in spending to create jobs he gave New York a lot of improvements that it badly needed—parks, roads, schools, reservoirs, and the like. Also he discovered two assistants, both social workers, who were to stay with him: a man, Harry Hopkins, and a woman, Frances Perkins.

The depression continued to go down and down, and a terrified country began to fear that it had no bottom. In 1930 the Democrats won a majority of the Senate, and the Republicans held the House by only two votes, which meant that they had no effective control of Congress.

Yet if they had held Congress the victory might have done them no good, for a Congress without leadership from the White House seldom accomplishes anything important. Hoover seemed to have run completely out of ideas, which is strange, because in business he had been full of them. Before he went into politics he was a mining engineer and was said to have made ten million dollars because he could always think of something when everybody else was stuck. At the start of the First World War, before we got in, he was given the very delicate task of administering American aid to the starving Belgians, and he made a wonderful record by his ingenuity in getting things done.

But in both business and war relief he had operated under a set of rules that were made before he was born. He could stretch them and get around them, but he never broke them; and he perhaps could not even imagine a situation in which there simply weren't any rules, because the old ones had vanished and new ones hadn't been made. But the depression was just such a situation, and as 1932 approached most observers became convinced that he would not be elected President again. The Republicans had to renominate him, for to do anything else would be to admit that they had misled the country, and no politician would think of taking that stand. But plainly, by the beginning of the year, any first-rate Democrat was going to be able to beat him.

The great victory in the New York election of 1930 convinced both Roosevelt and Howe that if he were ever to strike for the biggest political prize of all, now was the time. Several prominent Democrats had won in that year, but no other had made such a record as that of Roosevelt in New York.

As for the sad state of the Republican party, it was, of course, a help, but it was also a danger to Roosevelt. By January, 1932, politicians could see that a great many Americans were going to vote against Hoover. Some blamed him for bringing on the depression, which was unfair; but others were against him because he had not found, and they did not think he would ever find, means of checking the depression. That criticism was reasonable. Either way a great many of these people were strictly against

Hoover. They were not for anybody else. Whoever opposed Hoover would get their vote.

The effect of this situation was to add great value to the Democratic nomination. In 1928, it hadn't been worth much, because the party was still in fragments, and Hoover still had the reputation of being one of the wisest men in the world. But now that the party was in better shape and Hoover was being blamed for everything, the nomination was a real prize, and every prominent Democrat in the country wanted it. All over the nation favorite sons began to pop up. A favorite son is a politician, usually a governor or a Senator, who is popular in his own state, but not very well-known outside. An example was Albert C. Ritchie, who had been elected governor of Maryland four times. The Maryland delegation to the national convention always voted for him on the first ballot, and the orators referred to him as "the favorite son of Maryland." There was always a chance that the convention would become deadlocked between the leading candidates and finally turn to a favorite son.

In 1932 the leading candidates were Alfred E. Smith and Franklin D. Roosevelt, both of New York, and the chance of a deadlock between them seemed good, so favorite sons sprouted in unusual numbers. Observers generally agreed that Smith would hold the City of New York, but Roosevelt had strong friends in the rest of the state, especially one named James A. Farley, who turned out to be one of the smartest politicians in America. So the New York delegation would be split, which meant a chance for favorite sons.

Now those years of letter writing began to pay off. In all the United States there was hardly a Democratic county chairman who hadn't had a letter from Roosevelt, so at least local leaders knew he was alive. Many of them had had several letters, giving sound advice about party affairs, so they knew not only that he was alive, but that he was a shrewd politician. Many of them were pledged to favorite sons, especially in the South and West, and they felt that if their favorite son couldn't get the nomination, they would take Roosevelt, but they wouldn't take Smith. Others were like the Marylanders who, if they couldn't nominate Ritchie—which they never really expected to do—would take either Smith or Roosevelt. In short, Roosevelt was the first choice of a considerable number of delegates, the second choice of twice as many, and the third choice of practically everybody. Three ballots showed that no favorite son had a chance, so on the fourth the Democrats nominated Franklin D. Roosevelt for President of the United States.

The cheering of the Roosevelt men had hardly died down when the convention was subject to an electric shock. The nominee was flying from Albany to Chicago to accept the nomination from the platform of the convention.

This appearance was startling, because the custom had always been for the candidate to pretend that he didn't know what was going on at the convention. It was silly, for everybody knew that he had been working frantically for months to get the nomination, and he had kept in touch, by telegraph and telephone, with his floor leaders during all the balloting. But this pose was the custom, and nobody dared drop it merely because it was all buncombe. So some days, or some weeks, after the convention adjourned, a committee of dignified stuffed shirts proceeded to the candidate's home and, in a long, windy speech, solemnly notified him that he had been nominated. Then the candidate, in an even longer and windier speech, thanked the committee, thanked the convention, thanked the party, and thanked his loyal friends for this great honor they had seen fit to confer upon him. After his acceptance, the formal campaign began.

But here was a candidate who dumped all that folderol in the ash can and went straight to business. Air travel was

Roosevelt with John Nance Garner (third from left) and son James (first from right) on board campaign train, Topeka, Kansas, 1932

still something of a novelty in 1932, as that red automobile had been in 1910, and conservative politicians were a bit doubtful about it, but it attracted attention.

Then, with the convention still in session, the candidate appeared on the platform and launched into a thundering campaign speech. He denounced all the doings, and still more the nondoings, of the Republicans for the past four years. He described the desperate plight of the unemployed, of the farmers, and of businessmen, especially small businessmen. And he wound up with a sentence that gave the party a new battle cry: "I pledge you, I pledge myself, to a new deal for the American people." From that moment the New Deal became the description of the Democratic party as the Happy Warrior had been the description of Al Smith four years earlier.

Unfortunately, the Warrior was not a bit happy now, and one can easily see why. Al Smith had served the Democratic party to the best of his ability, and he had served it well. His honesty, his energy, his strong common sense, and his superb courage had made him a splendid governor and a great party leader. In 1928 he had fought the party's battle against hopeless odds and suffered defeat when no man could have won. Still it was defeat, and now that the odds were better he felt that the party owed him a chance to make a comeback. When he was denied that chance, he thought that he had been given a dirty deal and he was bitter about it.

Up to this point one can sympathize with Al. But he did not stop at this point. If the party had thrown him down, he felt sure that somebody had schemed to do so. He would not admit, even to himself, that the party had a right to reject him for something that was not his fault, but that made him a risky candidate. Therefore, he decided that he had been betrayed, and who was more likely to have done so than the man who had won the nomination? The fact that Roosevelt had showed him up so badly in New York in 1928 made him all the more likely to be the villain behind the plot.

But the cold-blooded politicians who had most to do with running the party did not see the situation that way. They knew that religious prejudice existed, and they knew that it had cost Al Smith a large number of votes in 1928; they figured it at about four million. Most certainly this prejudice was not Smith's fault, but it was not theirs either. Furthermore, while the odds were better, they were not so much better that they could risk handing four million votes to the Republicans. In this estimate, they figured correctly. Four million votes switched to Hoover would have defeated Roosevelt in 1932. Anyhow, with a man at hand against whom religious prejudice did not run, and one who had proved himself stronger than Smith in New York, they did not feel that the party owed so much to Smith that it was compelled to take the risk.

This analysis is not to say that Roosevelt's men didn't work against Smith in and before the convention. They certainly did. But that work was part of the game as Smith, like other politicians, had always played it. Any man who runs for office is going to be opposed by the friends of other candidates, and if anyone objected Smith himself might well have said, as Harry Truman did say many years later, "If you can't stand the heat, get out of the kitchen."

That convention was the test that exposed the basic flaw in Alfred Emmanuel Smith. He could dish it out, but he couldn't take it. He allowed his hatred of Roosevelt to fester until it destroyed his Democratic faith. Later he joined with a group of extreme conservatives, most of them rich and life-long Republicans, in what they called the Liberty League, which opposed every move made by a Democratic President. Even the three-times-defeated Bryan, when an abler Democrat was elected, supported him loyally. With half Smith's brains, Bryan proved himself the bigger man.

By rushing to Chicago to make the acceptance speech, Roosevelt proved again that he was the sort who, the instant the gong rang, came out fighting, and he never stopped for a moment until the dawn of election day. Poor Hoover was

Roosevelt campaigning in Elmgrove, West Virginia, October, 1932

completely outclassed. He hung on grimly, but he could do nothing more. As we look back on the campaign nearly forty years later, we can see that he didn't know quite what he was fighting. The curious thing is that neither did Roosevelt. He was hitting Hoover and the Republican party from every angle, but he had not yet quite sighted the real target, and he made one wild swing that he later had plenty of reason to regret. In a speech at Pittsburgh he criticized Hoover for reckless spending. He had in mind the immense sums the Reconstruction Finance Corporation had handed to big business, but he did not make his point clear. For years afterward his enemies continued to quote that speech, and it caused Roosevelt no little embarrassment.

But later in the campaign he made a speech to a club in San Francisco in which he explained the main lines that the New Deal was to follow. It got very little attention at the time, because most people thought it a rather dull discussion of the theory of government. Actually it was a new kind of politics and by far the most important speech he made.

Still, everything indicates that Roosevelt went through the campaign of 1932 not really knowing what he was fighting. He knew he was right in promising a new deal, but he had no idea how right he was, or how new his new deal would have to be. Maybe his not knowing was a good thing. If he had realized exactly what he was getting into, the knowledge might have chilled his nerve.

CHAPTER XIV

# THE NEW DEAL

As was expected, Roosevelt won the election easily. But as the system then was—it has been changed since—a President elected in November did not take office until March 4 of the following year, so for nearly four months Roosevelt had no job. Of course, he had a tremendous lot of work to do getting ready to take over. But early in February, realizing that this chance was his last for at least four years to take a vacation as a private citizen, he went to Bermuda for a couple of weeks, coming back and landing at Miami, Florida, on February 15.

With James A. Farley and Louis McHenry Howe, Roosevelt reading congratulatory messages, New York, November 9, 1932

If he had had any doubt that he was getting into a grim business, it ended right there. When his boat docked and he came ashore, shortly after dark, many Democratic bigwigs and also the usual crowd of spectators were there to welcome him. In this crowd was a wild fanatic named Zangara, and as Roosevelt's automobile began to move away, Zangara started shooting. He was a bad shot, perhaps because a woman bystander struck his arm. He fired six times before the police could seize him, killed the mayor of Chicago, and wounded two or three others, but missed Roosevelt. The attempted assassination was a near thing, though, and he wasn't even President yet. (The State of Florida sent Zangara to the electric chair for murdering the mayor.)

Being shot at, however, didn't give Roosevelt a hundredth part of the worry he felt over the way things were going in the country. They were going from bad to worse and, more than that, they were going faster and faster. Possibly by the time Roosevelt took office he would become President of a ruined country, so he began to write his inaugural speech with that eventuality in mind.

The gloomy prophets were right, all too right. In 1932 the whole amount of goods made in this country—industrial output—was only a little over half (fifty-six per cent) of what it had been three years earlier. Half as much work meant half as much pay, which meant that workers could buy only about half as much of the agricultural output. Manufacturers, merchants, and farmers all found themselves with goods they could not sell, and without selling they could not get money enough to buy raw materials. By the end of 1932 people were wondering whether any businessman could pay what he owed, and credit collapsed. Early in 1933 they began to suspect that even the banks could not pay, and by February they were taking their money out in vast quantities and hiding the cash somewhere. On February 14, the day before Zangara shot the mayor of Chicago, there was such a run on the banks in Michigan that the governor declared a bank holiday. But this holiday was not to celebrate anything, it was simply an excuse to give the banks a chance to collect enough of what was owed them to pay off the frightened depositors who were demanding their money. The next week the governor of Maryland declared a bank holiday, and state after state followed until banks were closed in twenty states. On March 3 the governor of New York declared a bank holiday, and that announcement put the lid on.

Roosevelt was inaugurated at noon on March 4, and he immediately did two things. He called the new Congress to meet five days later, and he declared a bank holiday for the whole country until Congress could meet. He certainly had a right to call Congress, but whether he had a right to declare a bank holiday was doubtful. That step however, was so plainly the only thing to do that not a bank in the country tried to open.

But Roosevelt also did a third thing that was more important than the other two. When he took the oath on the usual stand built on the steps of the Capitol, he faced the crowd standing in the square below and made a speech

Chief Justice Charles E. Hughes, Roosevelt, James Roosevelt, and former President Herbert Hoover (from left to right) at the inauguration on March 4, 1933, in Washington, D. C.

that, although it was not particularly eloquent, was, as far as its effect was concerned, the most tremendous speech ever delivered by an American President who was not asking for a declaration of war.

What he said was that there was in the country at that moment plenty of food, vast stores of grain, vast herds of cattle and hogs, and flocks of sheep and poultry. There were stores of cotton and wool to make clothing, huge supplies of leather for shoes, plenty of practically everything that people need to keep them healthy and strong. Yet millions were going hungry and ragged, not because of any shortage, but because men were afraid to try to move these stocks lest they become snarled in the tangle we had made of our monetary system. Fear, he said, nothing else, had paralyzed business and produced misery. Then he spoke words that went ringing through the country and have never been forgotten: "The only thing we have to fear is fear itself."

But the government he headed was not afraid of fear. It was going to get the goods moving and the needs of the people supplied. Ways and means of doing so, he would work out with the aid of Congress soon to assemble, but these things were going to be done, and if customs and traditions stood in the way, they would be trampled down. There was going to be action, and action now.

All over the country men said, "He's right. We *have* been seeing ghosts, and there's no sense in it. He's given us the word so let's go!"

So they went, and how! Congress met on March 9 and sat for ninety-nine days, in which time it passed more progressive legislation than had been enacted in the previous ninety-nine years. People whose minds turned to history remembered the number of tremendous events crammed into the period between Napoleon's return from Elba and the battle of Waterloo, a period just one day longer. So they gave to this session of Congress the name applied to Napoleon's second reign, and it has been known since as the Hundred Days.

Mistakes were made, and no miracles were worked, but the country got action, fast and furious action. After the creeping paralysis that it had suffered since 1929, any action was as stimulating to the economy as the wiggling of his big toe, after two years of effort, was stimulating to Roosevelt.

Moreover, in spite of many expensive errors of judgment and a few outrageous follies, the action was, on the whole, effective. That fact is plain because, after more than thirty years and several shifts of power from party to party, none of the chief laws enacted under the New Deal has ever been repealed. On the contrary, most of them have been strengthened and extended, usually by the Democrats, but more than once by the Republicans.

Now if this book were to try to explain all the things that were done by the New Deal, it would run into many volumes and would no longer be a story about Roosevelt, but a history of the United States. One thing, though, must be mentioned, because it was strictly Roosevelt's idea and shows what kind of man he was.

When he became governor of New York, at almost the worst part of the depression, he saw at once that if the state were to keep on the way it had been going, some people would starve to death and many would be brought so near starvation that they would become desperate and take to stealing and looting stores and fighting the police when opposed. There would be riots and bloodshed and such a breakdown of government that nobody would be safe. This situation had already begun to happen in the Middle West, where judges had been pulled off the bench to keep them from ordering foreclosures, a legal order by which creditors can take a man's land if he doesn't pay his debts. There dairy farmers, who could get next to nothing for their milk, had started such serious riots that some governors had to call out the National Guard to keep the peace.

This sort of thing couldn't be allowed to happen in New York, but to prevent it Governor Roosevelt had to learn the exact facts, which he found hard to do. Many of the politicians in public office didn't know the facts, and some who did were afraid to report them because they were so bad that to admit them would anger their bosses and maybe cost them their jobs.

So Roosevelt looked around for people who knew the truth and couldn't be punished if they told it. He found that in the colleges and universities were many men who had spent years studying these very problems and were willing to tell him the truth, because they held no political jobs and so couldn't be fired by some politician. They proved very helpful.

Then, when he was nominated for President, he realized that in the campaign he was going to have to discuss many of the same kind of problems, but forty-eight times as big, because many of New York's troubles were troubling all the other states. Immediately he turned to the colleges again, but this time instead of calling in two or three from New York institutions, he sent anywhere in the country for any man who had made a reputation as a master of some subject with which he had to deal. Veteran newspapermen who had watched around political headquarters until they knew every prominent politician in the country were amazed by the number of strangers showing up at Roosevelt's place.

One reporter was so impressed that he wrote his paper

that Roosevelt seemed to be trying to get a monopoly of all the brains in the country. Remembering the oil, beef, sugar, tobacco, and other monopolies that Theodore Roosevelt had fought, he said that this Roosevelt was about to set up a Brains Trust. The country laughed, and the phrase, without the *s,* caught on. Roosevelt's advisers were thereafter known as the Brain Trust. When he was elected, he took many of them to Washington, and some, for instance Professors Raymond Moley and Rexford Tugwell, he appointed to high office; he also brought in many younger faculty men to head the new agencies he was setting up. No earlier President had gathered around him so many men with the Ph.D. degree.

One wonders what there was in Roosevelt's life that made him take a line never followed by any other President, a line that many professional politicians regarded as foolish. No one can answer that question with certainty, but we do know that when any man has had to face truth that is not merely unpleasant, but dreadful, the confrontation does something to him that lasts. If he is a weak character to begin with, it may drive him out of his mind. But if he is a strong character, he will thereafter not hesitate to face less terrible truth promptly.

When he came down with polio, Roosevelt came face to face with death and with what was more appalling to him, life as a helpless invalid. He escaped death, but invalidism he could not escape, and if he was not helpless it was because of his steel-hard determination not to be helpless. When he became President and all experts agreed that the country

Franklin and Eleanor Roosevelt leaving Warm Springs
for Washington, D. C., December, 1933

was in great danger, his answer was, "Well, let us first find out exactly what the danger is, and exactly how great it is, and then pull the country out." That attitude would account for his reliance on men who might not know much politics, but who were skilled at finding exact facts, no matter how unpleasant they might be.

CHAPTER XV

# OPPOSITION, HOME AND ABROAD

The New Deal, by facing the facts and acting accordingly, did relieve some of the people's woes and, therefore, was immensely popular. When Roosevelt came up for reelection in 1936 every state in the Union voted for him except Maine and Vermont, and the vote in the electoral college was 523 to 8.

Yet despite its great successes in some things, the New Deal failed in the greatest test of all. It delivered Americans from the threat of starvation, but it did not deliver them from the threat of destruction by violence. On March 3,

1933, the day before Roosevelt became President of the United States, the new chancellor of Germany, Adolf Hitler, was voted power to suspend the constitution and the laws. This act of the German Reichstag made Hitler the dictator of Germany. His purpose was to destroy political liberty, because he did not consider ordinary men capable of governing themselves.

Few believed this, although there was no secret about his plans. Hitler had announced frankly what he wished to do in a book published several years earlier. Its title was *My Battle* (in German, *Mein Kampf*), and it was written while he was in jail for having tried to overthrow the German republic. But not many people read the book when it first came out, and of those who did most took it for the raving of a crazy man. Millions read it later, but then it was too late.

Not even after Hitler had proved his power to excite a German crowd into such a frenzy that they lost their heads completely did the rest of the world pay much attention. Americans, like others, thought that Hitler was only trying to win votes by his violent speeches. They thought that even if he did believe the things he said, no civilized nation in the twentieth century would follow him for long.

There is no reason to think that Roosevelt, in 1933, believed Hitler any more than the average American did. But soon after he became President our people abroad—diplomats, military attachés, and foreign service men—began to send in news that seemed to show that Hitler really was going to start a war. In Italy Benito Mussolini had done so; he had conquered Ethiopia. But Italy was a relatively weak power, so he wasn't much of a threat to France or Russia. Hitler, however, was in command of a strong and vigorous nation, which made him very different from Mussolini.

The President of the United States has people all over the world whose business it is to tell him what is going on. Every ambassador or minister plenipotentiary has a number of assistants, first, second, and third secretaries, military attachés, a press officer, interpreters if the country is not English-speaking, consuls, and special agents of various departments, especially the Treasury, Commerce and Justice, all of whom report anything of interest in the place to which they are assigned. This network makes it possible for the President to know more about what is going on in the world than any other man in the country can know.

Most of this information he immediately hands on to Congress, and much of it to the public through the newspapers. But sometimes he learns things that, if made public, would embarrass and perhaps endanger some friendly nation. Such things he keeps to himself. Sometimes he learns things that need to be known only by the Secretary of Defense and the commanders of the armed forces. This information he tells to those persons who ought to know it, but not to anyone else. If the President blurted out everything he knows, he could cause any amount of trouble and might bring the country into serious danger.

All this explanation is fairly simple. Any man of good sense, President or not, knows that there are times when one should keep his mouth shut. The real problem arises when the President learns something that the whole country ought to know, but that is so startling that few will believe it. If he tells it without proof that it is so, the people will not believe him and will lose confidence in anything he says. If he has proof and offers it, he may shock the country into doing something hasty and unwise. His best course is to let the news out gradually so that the country will become accustomed to it bit by bit. But this procedure takes time, and often there isn't enough time.

Before the end of 1935, the news that his men were sending from Europe convinced Roosevelt that Hitler's National Socialist Party (called Nazi for short) really intended to destroy democratic government, if it could, and bring all the world under the rule of the master race, which meant, of course, the Germans. Those nations—as, for example, Mussolini's Italy—that chose to assist the *herrenvolk* (German for master race) would be allowed a certain amount of freedom, but others must submit or be destroyed.

If the President himself couldn't believe the reports at first, how could he expect the ordinary American, with not a tenth of his information, to believe them? Plainly he didn't believe them in 1933, nor perhaps in 1934; if he had, he would not have spent all his time and energy on such problems as the unemployed, and unfair business practices, and the danger of soon finding everything in the country owned by a few men. These things needed attention, certainly, but improving the republic was hardly worthwhile, if the republic itself were presently to be wiped out.

So as early as 1935 Roosevelt started the business of letting the news out gradually. In this year he gave what is remembered as the I-hate-war speech. The gist of it was that he, who had been there in 1919 and had seen what the First World War had done to Europe, would forever after hate war. Yet if the nation should be drawn into war again, it should be ready with the men and the weapons, and especially it should now, in time of peace, be making friends who could be relied on to help it in case war came. Its natural friends were the other free nations.

Roosevelt didn't hope that everybody would agree with that speech, but he was astonished by the fury that it aroused. A large number of Americans believed that for any statesman to mention war would help to bring on war, and Roosevelt had not only mentioned it, he had suggested that we ought to be prepared for it in case it came. He thought this policy was nothing new. As far back as the days of ancient Rome wise men had been saying, "In time of peace prepare for war," but after the First World War a great many Americans had become convinced that preparing for war brings on war. Therefore, any statesman who so much as mentioned the possibility of another war was, as some men said, an enemy of the people. When Roosevelt mentioned it, his opponents denounced him so furiously that, for a time, he dropped the subject.

By then he had plenty of opposition for reasons not involved with the question of war and peace. Some criticism he deserved, for the New Deal made many mistakes, some of them bad ones. For instance, the first scheme to put great numbers of people back to work—it was called the Public Works Administration—was badly mismanaged. The idea was that since private business had stalled, public projects of all kinds should be increased. For that purpose, the Federal government would supply the money; but, since Washington couldn't know what every village and town needed, the money would be given to local officials, governors, mayors, city councils, county commissioners, and so on, to use as they saw fit. But these men were mostly small-time politicians, some of them with little brains and less character. Some saw fit to put the money in their own pockets and many used it to help their political friends, but not their enemies. Millions were stolen, and hundreds of millions wasted in the PWA. It had to be abandoned, and the same object sought through another agency, the Works Progress Administration, with authority to spend the money itself on something worthwhile.

Then the effort to do away with unfair business practices blew up, because it was based on the wrong idea. This idea was that the leaders in each industry should get together and work out a code of fair practice that all would honor. The plan failed, because some business leaders flatly refused to agree to honor the code and others adopted trick codes that gave somebody an unfair advantage. When the Supreme Court finally declared the whole idea unconstitutional, a good many New Dealers were glad.

A man could dislike these things and criticize Roosevelt for his part in them, and still be a reasonable man. But they were no excuse for hating him, and they were not the reason for the hatred that began to be directed at Roosevelt. The reason was fear. Not everybody was jobless and hungry and ragged on account of the depression. Some were doing very well under the old system, which they called capitalism, and many of these men were honestly afraid that Roosevelt was bent on destroying it. He told them over and over that he was not trying to destroy capitalism, that he was trying to strengthen it by bracing up the weak spots. But that explanation seemed to them merely an excuse. The weak spots were not bothering them, so they saw no need for such a tremendous lot of bracing up. Roosevelt was himself a capitalist, who had lived most of his life on the income from investments. Nevertheless, his critics made up their mind that he was an enemy of capitalism; if not an actual Communist, he was still something very much like one. Having made up their minds, they would no longer listen to reason and denounced not only the mistakes but also the good things that the New Deal was doing.

But the mass of the people didn't feel that way. Most of them had only a vague idea of what capitalism was, anyhow. All they saw was that Roosevelt was working hard to get them jobs and to put enough money in their pockets to keep them from starving. So what anybody called him made no difference, the people were for him. Only when he mentioned war did they suddenly become afraid. He realized how they felt, so after the I-hate-war speech he said no more about war for several months.

Still, Roosevelt kept getting news from Europe that was more and more alarming. In 1931 the Spaniards had thrown out their king and set up a republic, but in 1936 a Spanish general named Franco started a revolt against the republic. At first most Americans thought that he meant to bring back the king, but in time they learned that he cared nothing about the king, he simply wanted to destroy government by the people. Hitler and Mussolini, of course, were glad to help him, and did so, with great quantities of arms, ammunition, and especially with bombs and fighting planes. France and Russia gave some help to the republic, although most Americans believed that Russia helped in the hope of making Spain a Communist country. After three years of bitter fighting, in which a million people died, Franco beat down the republic and, thereafter, ruled Spain himself, instead of bringing back the king.

Great Britain and the United States did nothing except hamper the republic by refusing to give or sell it arms. The United States even seized the money that the republic had deposited in American banks. We did not hate the republic, but we feared to be drawn into another European war. Congress passed a series of so-called neutrality acts that were not neutral but helpful to Franco by preventing the republic from getting aid from us.

Roosevelt knew that this policy was all wrong, but he couldn't persuade the country. In 1937 he made another speech, as Hitler and Mussolini were helping Franco batter down the Spanish republic. He suggested that the peace-loving nations ought to seal off the war-like—"quarantine the aggressors" was his phrase—so as to cut down their ability to fight. But the outcry after the Quarantine speech was even louder than the one after the I-hate-war speech.

Roosevelt subsided. On this matter he couldn't persuade

the country to follow him, even though he was the finest persuader the country had seen in many years. Yet he knew that there is much truth in the philosopher Santayana's remark that any people who will not learn history are doomed to repeat it. We had not learned from the First World War—or, to be exact, we had learned too much that wasn't so. Few would admit the truth—that we had actually won a great victory for democracy, and then thrown it away because American politicians thought winning an election more important than defending liberty. To prevent Wilson and his party from gaining too much credit, they defeated the League of Nations, Wilson's plan for joint defense of liberty, and offered nothing in its place. Woodrow Wilson had said much the same thing during his final effort to save the League of Nations. He predicted that if the League was defeated, the country would have to fight another war at ten times the cost.

One thing that reduced Roosevelt's power over the people at this time was a political mistake that he made in 1937. Of the nine justices of the Supreme Court four were extreme conservatives and one, while less extreme, was inclined that way. A law suit takes from two to three years to work its way up from the lowest to the Supreme Court, so in 1935 and 1936 cases involving the important laws passed in the Hundred Days began to reach the high court. One after another the laws were struck down as unconstitutional, always by the same vote of five to four. There was a likelihood that all Roosevelt's work would go for nothing even though it had been approved by a tremendous vote of the people in the election of 1936, because five justices, all but one over seventy years old, did not approve. No matter if the President suggested, Congress passed, and the people supported a program of laws that they all deemed good and necessary, they could do nothing if five old men said, "No, the Constitution forbids such laws." Four justices did not agree. They saw nothing in the Constitution that forbade the kind of thing the New Deal had been doing, but they were only four to five.

All nine members of the Court had been appointed by earlier Presidents, going back to Wilson. Roosevelt privately thought, although to say so publicly would have been shocking, that the five conservatives were so old that their mental powers were failing. He, therefore, proposed that Congress enact a law providing that when a justice of the Supreme Court reached the age of seventy and chose not to retire, the President might appoint a younger justice, provided the whole number of the court should never exceed fifteen.

The idea itself was not bad, but the fact that it came from the President was bad—a good deal worse than Roosevelt realized. Most men at the age of seventy can no longer do either the hard work or the hard thinking that they could do at, say, thirty-five. But this decline does not always happen. Mr. Justice Holmes retired at ninety-one, and he was still one of the finest judges on the Court. So was Mr. Justice Brandeis, at eighty-three. Still, these exceptions did not disprove the rule. Most men are not good judges, any more than they are good soldiers, in extreme old age.

The real objection to Roosevelt's scheme was that it

would have given the President power to threaten the Court if he did not like its judgments, and most Americans didn't think he should have such power. He already had power to appoint the justices—if the Senate consented, which it nearly always did. But once appointed, neither Congress nor the President had any more power over the justice unless he committed a crime, such as taking a bribe or betraying the country. Since no justice had ever done so, the Supreme Court had always been independent of the executive and the legislative, as the Constitution makers intended it to be.

Other things helped to defeat the scheme. About this time the four liberal justices persuaded one of the five conservatives to come over to their side, and the Court began to sustain New Deal laws as regularly as it had been striking them down. Congress passed a law allowing a justice to retire on full pay at the age of seventy, and two of the conservatives soon took advantage of it. Thus Roosevelt was able to appoint two new men in the regular way, and he no longer needed the proposed change to prevent the defeat of his whole program. Eventually he appointed all but two members of the Court, and one of the two, Harlan F. Stone, he raised from associate to chief justice.

But the damage was done. He had given his enemies a weapon, and a deadly one, to use against him. They could accuse him of trying to destroy the independence of the Supreme Court, and his friends couldn't make any strong defense.

This proposal was the worst political mistake that Roosevelt ever made, and its bad effects showed up almost at once. A new Congress was to be elected the next year, 1938, and Roosevelt decided that the time had come to get rid of those Democrats who from the start had been opposing nearly everything he did. They were men of the Al Smith type of mind—unable to believe that as times change, we must change with them. They believed that Roosevelt was aiming, not to reform, but to destroy capitalism, and the more he succeeded the more determined they became in their opposition. Most of them, especially those from the South, were old-style Democrats who thought that what was sound policy in Grover Cleveland's day was still sound in Roosevelt's day, and anybody who disagreed was certainly tainted with socialism and maybe with communism.

Roosevelt tried to defeat these Congressmen in their home states. This strategy would have been dangerous at any time, for when a President interferes in a state election the voters usually resent him. Still, if Roosevelt had been at the very height of his popularity, he might have succeeded, at least in part. But he was fatally weakened by the Supreme Court fight. His enemies were able to claim that, not content with trying to take control of the Supreme Court, he was now trying to take over Congress too. The outcome was that with the exception of one Representative from New York, every man that Roosevelt opposed was triumphantly reelected.

These two defeats reminded him sharply of something that a successful leader is very likely to forget. While a man can't be a leader unless he is out in front, he must never get so far in front that he is out of sight. A man who gets too far in front cannot lead, any more than one who falls too far behind. When Roosevelt talked about the depression, for instance, the people believed him and were ready to follow him, for they had all felt the depression, and they knew that what he said about it made sense. But when he talked of something they had not felt directly, such as the danger presented by reactionary judges, or the mortal enmity to liberty of the Fascist idea, they were suspicious and responded slowly.

The response to the I-hate-war speech and then to the Quarantine speech taught him that the mounting threat of Hitlerism had not yet been perceived by the American people. Then defeats in the Supreme Court fight and the purge of Congress showed him the limits of his powers of persuasion. Evidently in dealing with foreign affairs he was very far in advance of public opinion. Therefore, he had better walk slowly and carefully. This situation was reality. Whether good or bad, it was the fact and must be faced.

CHAPTER XVI

# NEUTRALITY

In 1938 Roosevelt was halfway through his second term, and everybody supposed that two years later he would retire. There is no doubt that, at least until the end of 1937, he thought so too. No law said he must, but George Washington, who could easily have been elected a third time, refused. He had good reason to do so. Out of the previous twenty years he had spent eighteen in one public job or another—member of the Continental Congress, commander of the Army, presiding over the Constitutional Convention, President—and these jobs had just about ruined him. If his wife,

Martha, had not been an unusually good manager of the plantation at Mount Vernon, he would have been ruined. So he claimed the right to quit.

Thomas Jefferson could have been elected a third time, and he also refused. As a matter of fact, at the end of eight years he was sick of the job, but he said that since the great and wise Washington had refused a third term, he, Jefferson, would do likewise. These two men set the example, and no President following them served three full terms.

As far as domestic issues were concerned, Roosevelt could turn the job over to someone else in 1940 and be reasonably sure that the work would go on. This fact was so plain that several prominent New Dealers began to get ready to take over. James A. Farley, for instance, who was Roosevelt's best political aid, began quietly lining up delegates, and so did several others. In theory, Roosevelt should have stopped them before they made themselves ridiculous; but in practice he couldn't stop them without announcing that he would run again, and he still didn't know that he ought to, or, indeed, that he could.

The no-third-term tradition was very strong—so strong, indeed, that many Americans thought it was part of the Constitution. More than that, Stalin, Hitler, Mussolini, Franco, and a dozen rulers of smaller countries had shown how easily a man in power could make himself a dictator. If Roosevelt ran a third time, he would certainly be accused of aiming at becoming a dictator, and some people would believe the charge, perhaps enough to defeat him and elect a Republican who would try to undo all that the New Deal had done. A try for a third term would be very risky, even for a man with Roosevelt's enormous popularity.

On the other hand, Roosevelt was facing a fact that most of the American people did not suspect, and that he had not been able to explain to them. It was the fact that while he had been spending nearly all his time and energy fighting the depression, a more terrible threat was building up behind him. Of course, everybody knew that the countries called totalitarian, the Fascist, Nazi, and Communist countries, were opposed to government by the people and had done away with it within their own borders. Everybody knew, also, that in Fascist Italy, Nazi Germany, and Communist Russia, many who had dared speak for freedom had been butchered.

Yet a great many Americans couldn't see that this situation was any affair of ours. If the Germans, the Italians, and the Russians wanted that kind of government, so be it. Setting them free was not up to us if they didn't want to be free. Hitler knew that the way to keep the great numbers of people who do not think much on your side is to give them something to hate. So he picked on the German Jews, whom he blamed for everything that had gone wrong in Germany. He began to persecute them terribly, although he had not yet begun to murder them by wholesale—that development was to come later. Americans didn't like this behavior. They thought it was beastly. But the victims, after all, were not American citizens and had no claim on our government. As the British playwright, Shaw, said, "They were *his* Jews," and if he was fool enough to destroy valuable people, why should Britain try to stop him?

A few wise men, Roosevelt among them, knew that Hitler would not stop with the Jews or the Germans. He based everything on the theory that the people are not capable of governing themselves, and he had to prove it, first in Germany, but then in the nations surrounding Germany, and so on, until he brought the whole world under tyranny. He had to conquer completely, for if he couldn't destroy liberty everywhere, liberty somewhere would certainly destroy him. But to make the American people understand this fact was more than Roosevelt, or anybody else, could manage.

Nor were the Americans the only ones who didn't understand. The British and French were as bad. To stop Hitler meant risking another war with Germany, and the people of the democracies couldn't—or their leaders thought they couldn't—face up to that challenge. Hitler said that if they gave him what he wanted in central Europe, he would be satisfied. They believed him for one reason only: they wanted to believe him. So at a conference at Munich in September, 1938, the premier of France and the prime minister of Great Britain agreed not to interfere if Hitler seized the western half of the republic of Czechoslovakia, and the British prime minister, whose name was Chamberlain, came back to London saying that he had achieved "peace in our time."

The more intelligent people in Great Britain knew that

he hadn't, especially a member of the House of Commons named Winston Leonard Spencer Churchill. Roosevelt knew he hadn't. A large part of the American people were doubtful. However, there were many who were determined to believe that these people were in some kind of conspiracy to drag us into war to save Great Britain and France, not to defend ourselves. Some like Charles A. Lindbergh, for instance, believed that Hitler could beat us. A national hero since he had become the first man to cross the Atlantic alone in a single-engined plane in 1927, Lindbergh visited Germany in 1937, where they made much of him and showed him some of their new fighter and bomber planes. He was greatly impressed and came home with two fixed ideas, both wrong. One was that no nation could stand up against the German air force. The other was that air power could break the will to fight of any nation.

These two delusions convinced Lindbergh that if the United States were drawn into war against Germany the country would take a terrible beating. So he made speeches all over warning against having any part in the war, which he admitted was coming. Because Lindbergh was not a politician and had nothing to gain, whoever was in power, many of his hearers were persuaded that he was right. But he overshot the mark in a speech at Des Moines, Iowa, when he said something that sounded as if he were trying to excuse Hitler's persecution of the Jews. Of course, that statement infuriated all the Jews in the country, and non-Jews lost confidence in a man who made excuses for that kind of thing. From that time on Lindbergh was not very effective.

President Roosevelt addressing a joint session of Congress,
Washington, D. C., September 21, 1939

But others were, and their efforts forced Roosevelt to move very carefully. The break came on August 23, 1939, when Hitler and Stalin, supposed to be mortal enemies, made a deal by which each agreed not to attack the other and to act together if either were attacked by a third power. That pact was what they announced publicly, but nobody was fooled; what they had agreed on privately was to divide Poland between them, Germany taking the western and Russia the eastern half. Britain and France, who had guaranteed the safety of Poland, reminded Hitler and Stalin of that commitment, but Hitler paid no attention. Eight days later his army crossed the line into Poland, and the war was on.

From the very start Roosevelt knew that our only chance of keeping out was for the democracies to win a quick victory, and he very much doubted that they could do so. This estimate was evident to him for two reasons, one known to everybody, but the other known only to the relatively few people with a clear understanding of international affairs. Everyone knew that a long war would cause enormous destruction of the wealth of the world. Millions of tons of steel would be made into shells and bombs that would be exploded into fragments or into ships that would be sunk. Food, clothing, oil, coal, rubber, copper, and tin would be consumed in enormous quantities. But through the long, only partly successful, struggle of the New Deal against the depression Roosevelt had learned that the prosperity of America is so entangled with the rest of the world that it cannot be separated for any great length of time. Therefore, if the wealth of Europe were destroyed, the loss would fall heavily on us, and the fact must be faced.

But what other political leader knew the truth as well as the one who had learned it the hard way, by seven long years of struggle to restore the prosperity of one country in a world not yet recovered from the ruin of the First World War? Roosevelt did not believe there was any other man who had learned the true situation. Therefore, to take that hard-won, special knowledge away from the position where it could be used would be like running away as the danger was mounting. He would not do so. He would not ask for a third nomination, but he would not refuse if it were offered.

His enemies said this thinking was a lot of twaddle. He was a man so eaten by ambition and so in love with power that he could not bring himself to give it up. This accusation may have been true. Able men do love power and do hate to give it up, especially at a critical moment. On the other hand, men of sense know that to be President in critical times is a crushing burden, that any man of sense is glad to escape. So perhaps Roosevelt's reasons were exactly what he said they were.

At any rate, Roosevelt was renominated and reelected for a third term in 1940 against very powerful opposition. The Republicans, or at least their more intelligent leaders, realized that to run an old-style politician against Roosevelt would be to give away the election in advance, so they passed over the old party war-horses and looked around for the

Roosevelt campaigning for a third term, Newburgh, New York, 1940

kind of candidate who would be fresh and new. They settled on a man named Wendell Lewis Willkie.

The choice was a good one. Willkie had not been prominent in politics before 1940. Starting as a lawyer, he then got into the electric-power business. He had made millions by taking a number of small, more or less run-down, power companies and combining them into a huge network covering a number of Southern states, including Tennessee. There he ran head on into perhaps the most famous of all New Deal projects, the Tennessee Valley Authority. Among other things, the Authority was offering to supply cheap electric power to farmers, and Willkie's companies ran into competition with it. He fought and proved himself a first-class fighter. The TVA didn't want his power plants, but it did want some of his transmission lines, from which it proposed to lead others out into the country where Willkie's companies had never gone because there were too few customers. In the end, he made the TVA pay about twenty-three million more for his property than it had proposed, and Willkie became the hero of every big businessman in the country.

So he went into the campaign with two issues. First, he was going to stop this third-term nonsense. Second, he was going to stop government competition with private business.

But his issues didn't work. Willkie proved to be an excellent campaigner, and he was so transparently honest that he got the votes not only of all Roosevelt haters, but of some who rather liked the President, although they were disturbed by the third-term idea. Nevertheless, the war was on, Poland was being carved up, Britain and France were fighting. With all Europe going up in flames, why take a chance on a new and untried leader, third term or no? Then, as the matter turned out, Willkie's companies, far from being bankrupt, were making more money in the Tennessee Valley than they had ever made before. The TVA, by electrifying the farms, had created thousands of new customers, not only for power, but for electric refrigerators, washing machines, flat irons, and similar gadgets that the TVA didn't sell, but that Willkie's companies did. That development let the air out of the government competition issue.

So the election of 1940 went the usual way—Roosevelt won by a landslide. Still, Willkie cut Roosevelt's majority from eleven million in 1936 to a little less than four million in 1940. Where Landon, in 1936, got only eight electoral votes, Willkie got eighty-two, but Roosevelt held on to 449.

From the moment of his election in 1940 Roosevelt was a war President in all but name. He knew so, and the country knew so. The difference was that he was willing to face the fact, and the country, or at least its political leadership, was not. The United States was so big and so tied in with the rest of the world that it was bound to be drawn into any large-scale war. The best that Americans could do was to make sure that they fought on the right side.

Roosevelt had no doubt whatever that the democracies were on the right side, but he was far from certain that they were going to win, and he knew that he could not persuade the country to act. There were too many pacifists who held that in war there is no right side. Roosevelt, therefore, proceeded to do what he could indirectly. His enemies said that he acted illegally and in an underhanded fashion. He did not. From the very start he announced publicly that he was going to give the democracies all the aid that he could, short of war. Congress thought it had taken out of his hands power to do anything. But Roosevelt had shrewd lawyers who discovered a dozen ways to get around the neutrality acts, and more and more Congressmen were realizing that those acts had been a mistake from the start.

Then in 1940 Hitler, who for more than a year had been merely marking time while he got his army well-organized and properly placed, struck with all his power. The result was stunning. In three weeks the democracies were whipped. The immense French army turned out to be worthless. The men were brave enough, but the French generals, who had been great in the First World War, were not so now. Most of them were dead, and the others were so old and feeble that they were unfit to command a platoon of street sweepers, much less an army. The only younger ones who were any good were Colonel Jean Leclerc, who was far down in Africa, and Brigadier General Charles de Gaulle, who had a positive genius for rubbing everybody the wrong way. On the excuse that he was needed to confer with the British, he was sent to London to get him out of the way.

As for the civilian government, apparently half the politicians in it, led by the infamous Pierre Laval, were traitors, and the rest, with two or three honorable exceptions, were cowards. To make the surrender, they dragged out of retirement the ancient Marshal Henri Petain, who had been wonderful at Verdun, twenty years earlier, but whom age had enfeebled until he was really in his second childhood. Hitler contemptuously accepted Petain as the puppet governor of the southern part of France.

As for the British army, a third of it was destroyed and the rest flung out of Europe. It would have been captured completely except that the British people, civilians as well as naval and military men, took everything that would float across the English Channel and brought 300,000 men off the beach at Dunkirk.

Then Hitler made a mistake so gigantic that its like is hardly to be found in all history. He assumed that Britain was as completely whipped as France and that only mopping up remained. His intention had always been to cut the throat of his dear friend Stalin, and now seemed to be the time to do so. Accordingly, in September, 1940, he smashed the Russian army in Poland and sent it reeling back into its own country. That blow began a campaign equally disastrous to Napoleon's on the same ground in 1812.

Hitler left the mopping up of Britain to the man he had put in charge of his air force. This man, Hermann Göring, had promised so to soften Britain that the German army could land on the island with hardly the loss of a man. He was the one who had deceived Lindbergh into believing that he had an unconquerable air force. Now he hurled it against England, and it was hurled back in rags and tatters.

The British had developed the Spitfire, a fighter plane at least equal to anything Göring had, and they had also developed radar, so they could not be taken by surprise. They shot down German planes so fast that by the end of the month Hitler had to call off the operation, or he would have had no air force left.

The British also had another thing that Hitler did not understand. They had thrown out the bumbling Chamberlain and made Winston Churchill prime minister. From that time on, if he had only realized it, Hitler didn't have a chance.

Still Roosevelt's hands were tied. By this time he had no doubt whatever that if Hitler conquered all Europe he would attack this country, as Kaiser Wilhelm had attacked it by turning his submarines loose on our merchant ships. But he knew that a large number of Americans still didn't believe so, and to convince them was beyond his power. So he continued to do what he could indirectly. When Göring's air force was whipped, Hitler fell back on the old means of reducing Britain. He would use his submarines to sink every ship bound for Great Britain. German submarines could easily cross the Atlantic, so he could torpedo ships long before they got to Britain.

The best weapon against the submarine at that time was not the great battleship, but the small, very fast destroyer. Ever since the war started our Navy had been building destroyers at a furious rate. Whenever a new one was launched, an old one was taken out of service, but not turned over to the wreckers. The law forbade the Navy to

President Roosevelt signing the Lend Lease Bill,
Washington, D. C., March 11, 1941

sell any of its ships in service, but it could dispose of surplus property, so Roosevelt declared fifty of these destroyers "overage," and surplus. Then, as Britain had practically no dollars left, he did not sell, but swapped them for the right to build Naval bases on nine Atlantic and Caribbean islands owned by Britain. This famous Destroyer Deal infuriated his enemies, but there was nothing they could do about it.

As events proved, Hitler himself had arranged to solve Roosevelt's problem. He knew the danger of pushing the United States into the war, so he made a deal with the military gang that had gained control of the Japanese government. When his armies reached a certain point in Russia, which he thought would mean that Russia was defeated, Japan would attack the United States and keep us too busy to take a hand in Europe.

Three great German armies were driving into Russia, one aimed at Moscow, the capital, one at Leningrad, the great Baltic port, the third at Stalingrad, on the lower Volga River. This southern army had farther to go than the others, but in September, 1941, it arrived and laid siege to the city.

This critical moment required the last great effort, for when the three cities fell, according to the German theory, the war would be won. Therefore, Germany could not be distracted by a new threat from the West.

So, on December 7, 1941—"a day that will live in infamy," said Roosevelt—Japan struck.

CHAPTER XVII

# WORLD WAR II

From a carrier Japan sent over a hundred planes, and at 7:30 that Sunday morning they caught the American Pacific fleet of eighty-two ships lying at anchor in Pearl Harbor in Hawaii. In an hour and fifty minutes the bombers sent much of the fleet to the bottom of the harbor and put the rest out of action. We lost nearly 5000 men, killed and wounded, and except for a few scattered ships had no offensive sea power left in the Pacific.

The next day Germany and Italy declared war on the United States.

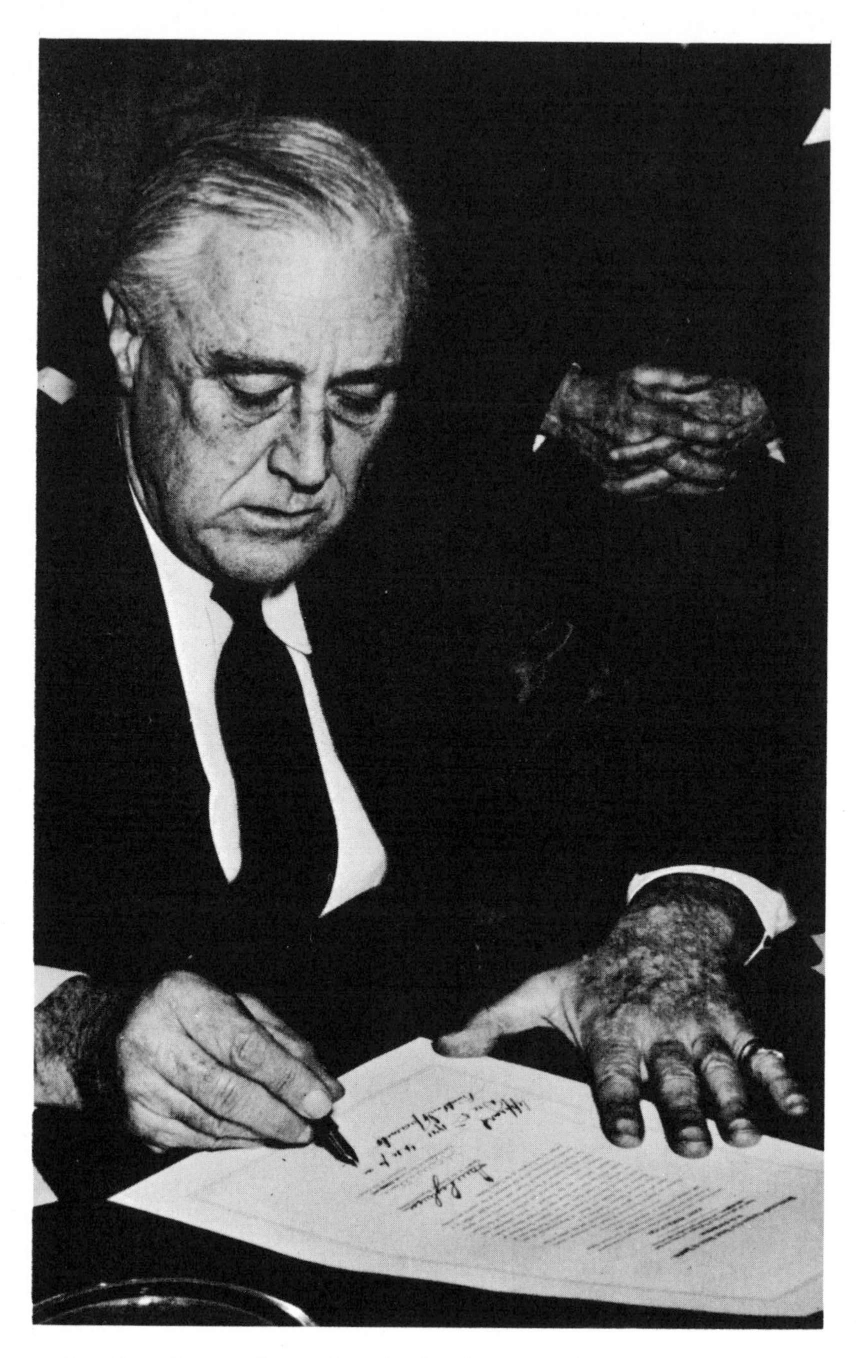

President Roosevelt signing the Declaration of War against Japan,
December 8, 1941

But the Americans didn't do what they were expected to do. Instead of spending all their time and energy on a hopeless effort to stop Japan in Asia, they threw everything they had to the support of Britain and Russia. America had nearly a million men in uniform, but transporting an army across the sea takes a long time. However, the country had vast quantities of food and supplies, which it started toward Europe instantly—guns, ammunition, tanks, trucks, tractors, blankets, tents, medicines, and in a very short time doctors and nurses. The Russians were still clinging desperately to their three cities, and the arrival of American supplies stiffened their resistance. Hitler's grand design had failed. Russia was not out of the war.

Furthermore, the British still had an army in the Near East composed of British, Indian, Australian, and New Zealand troops. The British navy could see that this army also got American supplies. It was supposed to be taken care of by the Italians in North Africa, but the Italians were not that good. They took a bad beating, and the British began to move from Egypt toward the French colony of Algeria, where they might have been able to do something to revive France. To stop them Hitler had to send a German army under one of his best generals, Erwin Rommel, soon to be known as the Desert Fox, although that army was badly needed in Russia.

The Americans now had an army and the ships to move it. The question was where to send it? There was tremendous pressure to send it to the Pacific where General Douglas MacArthur, who had been training the Philippine army, had been caught when the Japanese army swept down on the islands. Eight hours after Pearl Harbor the Japanese destroyed most of MacArthur's planes on the ground, so he was unable to prevent the landing of 40,000 Japanese troops against his 28,000. They drove him back along the Bataan Peninsula until he was pinned with the remnant of his army in the island fortress of Corregidor. His situation was hopeless, and at last, not of his own will but in obedience to a flat order from the President, he slipped out on a fast motorboat and reached Australia, where he was to organize a new army.

Many people, especially Senators and Representatives from the Western states, thought the country should send every available man to MacArthur. But the decision rested with the President as commander in chief, and he refused. There were two reasons for this strategy. In the first place, the way from Australia to the Philippines was mostly over water, which meant that it would be largely a Naval operation. In the second place, Roosevelt felt that tyranny must be broken at its strongest point, which was in Europe. Once Hitler was beaten, America could and would take care of Japan; but Hitler must be beaten first.

To MacArthur's friends this thinking seemed most unfair, and they complained loudly. But Roosevelt paid no attention. He had not made the decision entirely on his own. He had been wise enough, or lucky enough, to appoint two very great men to two extremely important positions. In supreme command of the Army, under the President, was George Catlett Marshall, and in command of the

General George Marshall, Roosevelt, Admiral Ernest King (seated left to right) Harry Hopkins, Lt. General H. H. Arnold, Lt. General Brehon Sommervell, Averell Harriman (standing left to right) at Casablanca, January 20, 1943

Navy, Ernest Joseph King. Neither General Marshall nor Admiral King was to lead a force in battle. But they chose the officers who were to lead, and without any important exception they chose well. These men agreed that the Army should be first thrown into Europe and the Navy into the Pacific.

King replaced the admiral who had been caught flat-footed at Pearl Harbor with Chester William Nimitz, one of the greatest Naval officers this country has ever produced. Marshall gave the Army to Dwight David Eisenhower, perhaps the only American general who could have fought the kind of war he had to fight. Nimitz had to collect a battle fleet, which took time. Eisenhower had to get the Army across the Atlantic, which also took time. Stalin, of course, was screaming for a landing in France to take the Germans in the rear and relieve the pressure on Russia. Churchill wanted a tactical diversion too, for the Germans were building the huge V-2 rockets with which they were to do great damage to English cities and kill a great many English civilians.

But Eisenhower wanted to test and train his soldiers in actual fighting before throwing them against the best of the German army. So the decision was to go first to the aid of the British Eighth Army in Africa, which Rommel had driven back almost to Cairo. The Americans were to land in West Africa, in the territory held by the French, their main force to occupy Casablanca, with smaller detachments

General Giraud, Roosevelt, Charles de Gaulle, and Winston Churchill at Casablanca, January 24, 1943

at several nearby ports. But just a week before the Americans took Casablanca the British Eighth Army turned on Rommel and, in a four-day battle at a place called El Alamein, smashed him and drove him headlong toward the west. At Casablanca the French were confused. They had no orders from Petain, and at the start fired on the Americans, but then thought better of their resistance and surrendered. The Germans, caught between Eisenhower and Alexander, the British commander, left Africa for Sicily. Eisenhower and Alexander followed, and drove them halfway up the Italian peninsula.

Then Eisenhower was ordered back to London to take command of the long-sought invasion of France. On June

General Dwight D. Eisenhower and Roosevelt in Sicily on December 8, 1943

6, 1944, he landed 176,000 men on the Normandy beaches, and as they pushed inland poured in others until he commanded more than two million men, with whom he fought the Battle of Normandy and the Battle of France, each of which was not a battle, but a campaign including a dozen fights bigger and bloodier than the Battle of Gettysburg. He swept the Germans out of France and plunged through Germany to meet the Russians at the Elbe River and take the surrender of Germany in exactly eleven months after the landing.

In the meantime, King had assembled a fleet for Nimitz, consisting in part of vessels raised from the bottom of Pearl Harbor and mended, but in part of fine, new ships, especially airplane carriers. Then followed the most tremendous naval war fought in modern times. Because it was so far away and reports were often so confused, most Americans had a very dim idea of what fierce fights were the Battle of Makassar Straits, the Battle of the Java Sea, the Battle of the Coral Sea, the Battle of Midway, the Battle of Savo Island, and so on, up to the Battle of Leyte Gulf, which finished the Japanese Navy. In two of them, the Java Sea and Savo, we were badly beaten, and several others resulted in a draw. But at Midway, just seven months after Pearl Harbor, the Japanese advance toward Hawaii was stopped cold. The United States Navy had revived.

Thereafter, Nimitz steadily gained and the Japanese steadily lost power. Immediately after Pearl Harbor they had rushed down the South Pacific, heading for Australia. They got as far as New Guinea, but there the Battle of

Roosevelt with General Douglas MacArthur and
Admiral Chester Nimitz at Pearl Harbor on July 26, 1944

Makassar Straits halted them, and a little later the Battle of the Coral Sea pinned them down. MacArthur moved up to New Guinea, and the Navy threw a division of marines onto Guadalcanal Island—nearly lost it, too, by the Battle of Savo Island—and held on until the Army could come up. After that, the process never halted. As fast as the sea around them was cleared of enemy fighting ships, MacArthur attacked the islands, except for some that he deliberately bypassed, knowing that with their supplies cut off they must surrender in time. Leyte Gulf is in the Philippines, and the battle there was a near thing, but the United States won it, and that victory was the end of the Japanese main fleet. MacArthur was back where he had started, and now he set out for Japan, which, after being hit with two atomic bombs, surrendered September 2, 1945.

This war was by long odds the biggest the United States

had ever fought. In fact, it was two wars waged at the same time, one in Europe, the other in the South Pacific. What won for the country was first, of course, the bravery and skill of its fighting men, but next the superb organization that put the fighters where they were needed and supplied them with weapons and food over immense distances. With the skill and courage of the men Roosevelt had nothing to do; but with the organization he had a great deal to do. He found the right men for the big jobs—not only Marshall and King, but dozens of others in less conspicuous posts. He kept politics from influencing the choice of generals. He helped Churchill keep de Gaulle in line on one side and Stalin on the other. Above all, he urged and encouraged the American people, especially the workers in the war industries. He was always good at talking to them, and never better than during the war years.

With victory coming in sight he was reelected for a fourth term in November, 1944. The election caused little excitement. The Republicans named a candidate, Thomas E. Dewey, but even Dewey himself probably had no real hope of winning. Americans weren't going to turn out a commander in chief in the midst of a war that he was plainly winning. His majority dropped to three and a half millions, but only because so many people didn't vote at all. Dewey got a quarter of a million fewer votes than Willkie had received in 1940.

The victory was empty, however. More than twelve years in the White House, five of them with the world in turmoil, and the last three with the United States fighting for its life,

Roosevelt with Winston Churchill and Joseph Stalin
at Yalta, February 9, 1945

had broken even such an iron man as Roosevelt. In February, he attended a final conference of the other war leaders at Yalta, in Russia, and when he returned he was plainly in bad shape. A few weeks later he was persuaded to go to Warm Springs, and there, on April 12, 1945, he suffered a stroke and died within two hours.

CHAPTER XVIII

# A GREAT PRESIDENT

Roosevelt faced the truth and made the rest of the country face it. That quality is his real claim to be called a great President. He had other qualities that were more shining and attracted more attention, but his ability to look unpleasant truth in the face was the great one. He had the quality that nobody can describe exactly, that we call charm. At the very darkest moment he could smile, and at most times he seemed to be gay and happy hearted. He was exceedingly quick at grasping an idea, and so could get through an enormous amount of work in a very short time.

He loved justice, although he was not always just, and he hated tyranny, although he was sometimes harsher than was necessary. He feared God, but neither man nor devil.

These qualities people could see and admire, and they made him immensely popular. But not until he was gone, and the great war was over, did Americans begin to realize fully that he was a patriot of the same kind as Nathan Hale, whose regret was that he had only one life to give for his country. The carefree manner was a mask. Behind it, the strain was wearing down even his rugged constitution, and eventually it killed him. He was a casualty of the war, as certainly as if he had been struck by an enemy bullet. But if he had served his country well, he accounted his life well sacrificed.

Americans should always remember, although few seem to, the debt they owe Winston Churchill in this matter. During the war, to hold the alliance together, the heads of the principal powers had to keep in close touch, so that each would know exactly what the others were doing. Radio and cables would serve, up to a point, but the best way was to talk face to face. Churchill, knowing that Roosevelt was a cripple for whom travel was difficult, time after time made the dangerous trip across the Atlantic to confer in Washington, or in Canada, risking his own life in consideration of Roosevelt's infirmity.

That Roosevelt was a great man there is no doubt whatever. Even those people who detest his memory—fewer, now, but a large number twenty years ago—admit that if he was not a great hero, he was certainly a great villain. He left behind him a country greatly changed from what it had been in 1932. His friends hold that it is, all things considered, a much better country. His enemies hold that it is much worse. But all hands agree that it is different. Most of the change, of course, was due to two forces that Roosevelt could not control: first the depression, and then the Second World War. But he also left behind a large number of new ideas about government and business. Not all of them were his own, but the way he explained them to the people put his stamp on them, so they will always be regarded as his.

Franklin and Eleanor Roosevelt leaving St. Thomas Church, Washington, D. C., April 13, 1941

So much is history, and it will be studied and argued over by historians as long as the nation lasts. He also left us something that is not exactly history but that will always interest Americans, especially young ones. He left us a story. It is more than a tale that is told just for fun; it is one of our legends.

To some this may seem a frivolous thing to mention about a President of the United States, but it isn't. A story, if it is really a stirring one, outlasts almost anything else in the world. Not for years, but for centuries, people have been listening to the stories of King Arthur and his knights, of Charlemagne and the Paladins, of Achilles and Ulysses, of Saint George and the Dragon.

Now nearly all the great old stories, whether they come from the Greek Iliad, the Arabian Nights, the French Song of Roland, or the English tales of the Round Table, have the same theme. They tell of some boy who seemed to be small and weak and of not much use. He went through many trials and dangers, sometimes beaten, often wounded, frequently escaping death by a hair; yet when the big test came he proved to be a Paladin, a Giant Killer, a Dragon Slayer, righter of wrongs and rescuer of the oppressed. When we have listened to such a tale, always interested, sometimes breathless, and at the end shake our heads and say, or at least think, "How I wish I could be a man like that," why then we may be sure that we have listened to a great story.

When one first looks at the story of Roosevelt's life, it may seem to break all the rules of heroic tales. According to the rule, Roosevelt should have begun as a poor orphan boy, without a friend, or a cent, or a roof over his head. As it was, he began as a rich kid, having everything that a Mama's darling could possibly need, and he went on as a young man, having a very easy life indeed, landing an excellent job mainly because of his prominent friends, winning high office mainly because his name was Roosevelt—all wrong as stories go.

Yet when the deadly disease struck, all that he had could not save him. His friends, his money, his honors, and dignities—none of them, nor all of them together, could give him back the strength of his legs or relieve the weight and pain of the steel braces when he tried to walk. From that time on, what counted was nothing that he had, but only what he was. And that is true of the heroes of all the great old tales. Achilles and Hector, King Arthur, Roland, the Paladin, and the Lion-Hearted—in every case, what the man was, not what he had, told the tale. The armor of Achilles, with Patroclus inside it, could not stop Hector. But Achilles stopped him. When he had nothing that could save him, Roosevelt saved himself; and that is exactly according to the rule.

For many years to come historians will still be disputing whether Roosevelt was right or wrong, in this or that. But long after the disputes have been settled, for as long as men still thrill to the story of one of their own kind whom misfortune could not break and danger could not appall, they will listen to the story of Roosevelt, and each will wish that he were such a man. Without doubt some, perhaps great numbers, who are themselves in pain and danger, remembering that those things, far from destroying Roosevelt, made him more of a man than he had ever been before, will take heart and nerve themselves to fight again.

This story is the one he left us and who will call it a little thing?

# INDEX

** Indicates illustrations*